HARCOURT
Science

Harcourt School Publishers

Orlando • Boston • Dallas • Chicago • San Diego

www.harcourtschool.com

Cover Image
The clownfish lives in tropical reefs of
the Pacific Ocean.

Printed in the United States of America

ISBN 0-15-311204-2

Authors

Marjorie Slavick Frank
Former Adjunct Faculty Member at
    Hunter, Brooklyn, and Manhattan
    Colleges
New York, New York

Robert M. Jones
Professor of Education
University of Houston-Clear Lake
Houston, Texas

Gerald H. Krockover
Professor of Earth and Atmospheric
    Science Education
School Mathematics and Science
    Center
Purdue University
West Lafayette, Indiana

Mozell P. Lang
Science Education Consultant
Michigan Department of Education
Lansing, Michigan

Joyce C. McLeod
Visiting Professor
Rollins College
Winter Park, Florida

Carol J. Valenta
Vice President—Education, Exhibits,
    and Programs
St. Louis Science Center
St. Louis, Missouri

Barry A. Van Deman
Science Program Director
Arlington, Virginia

★**3**

UNIT A

Life Science

Plants and Animals All Around

UNIT B

Life Science

Living Together

UNIT C

Earth Science

About Our Earth

UNIT D

Earth Science

Weather and the Seasons

UNIT E

Physical Science

Matter and Energy

UNIT F

Physical Science

Energy and Forces

★9

Using Science Skills

Observe

Compare

Sequence

8 days 22 days 35 days

Classify

Infer

Gather Information

Plan

Make Models

★13

Measure

Predict

Draw
Conclusions

Communicate

Science Safety

Think ahead.

Be neat.

Be careful.

Do not eat or drink things.

Safety Symbols

CAUTION

Be careful!

CAUTION

Sharp!

CAUTION

Be careful!

CAUTION

Wear an apron.

CAUTION

Wear goggles.

Plants and Animals All Around

UNIT A

Life Science

Plants and Animals All Around

UNIT PROJECT

Watch Me Grow!

Plan a class aquarium. Find out what things plants and animals need to live there.

Living and Nonliving Things

Did You Know?
Dogs have **senses**
as people do, but
dogs can hear
higher sounds.

Did You Know?
The oldest **living** thing on Earth is the bristlecone pine tree in the United States.

How Do My Senses Help Me Learn?

 Investigate

Using Your Senses

You will need

pieces of fruit

plastic gloves

1 Close your eyes. Your partner will put on gloves and give you a piece of fruit.

2 Touch and smell the fruit. Tell what you observe. Name the fruit.

3 Take turns with your partner.

Science Skill
When you observe things, use more than your eyes to find out about them.

Your Five Senses

You have five **senses** that help you learn about things. What part of your body do you use for each sense?

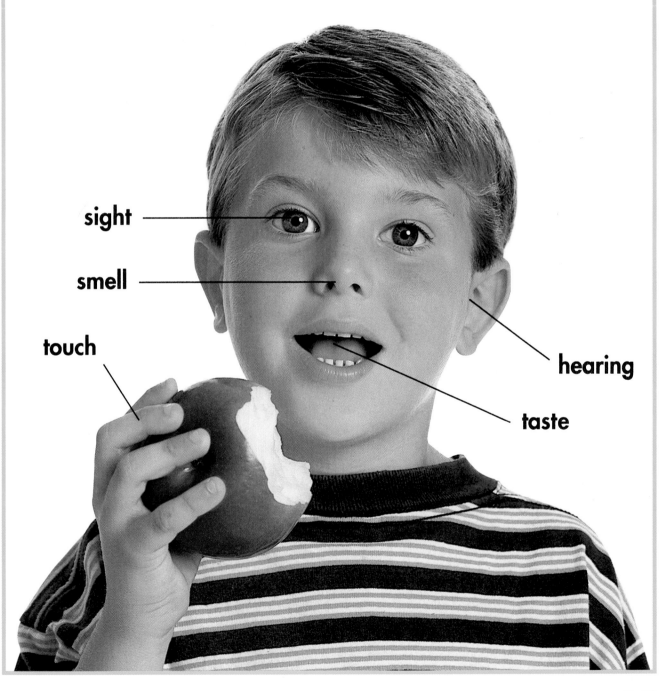

sight

smell

touch

hearing

taste

Sight

Your sense of sight helps you learn
how things look.

■ **What can the boy learn
by looking at the fish?**

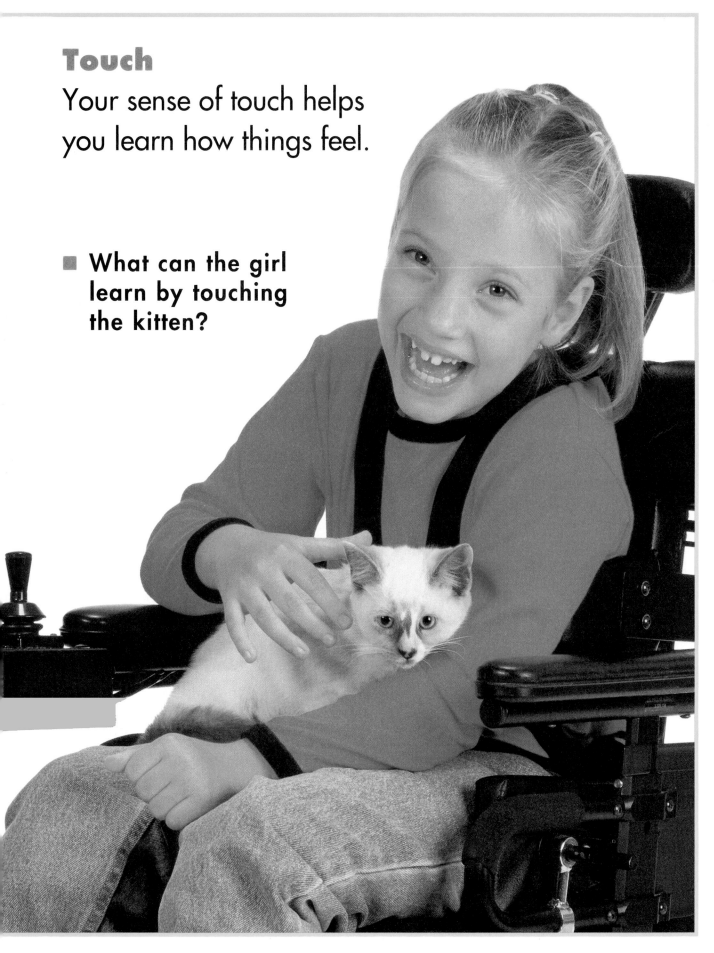

Touch

Your sense of touch helps you learn how things feel.

■ **What can the girl learn by touching the kitten?**

Hearing

Your sense of hearing helps you learn about sounds.

■ **What sound does this boy hear?**

Smell

Your sense of smell helps you learn how things smell.

- **How do you think these flowers smell?**

Taste

Your sense of taste helps you choose what to eat.

- **How do you think these grapes taste?**

Think About It

1. What are the five senses?
2. How do your senses help you learn?

What Are Living and Nonliving Things?

 Investigate

A Mealworm and a Rock

You will need

mealworm

rock

 hand lens

 bran meal

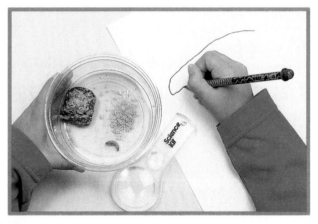

1 Give bran meal to the mealworm and the rock. Use the hand lens to observe.

2 Does the mealworm or the rock move or eat? Draw what you see.

3 Compare the mealworm and the rock. Which is a living thing?

Science Skill

When you compare things, you tell how they are the same and different.

Living and Nonliving Things

Plants, animals, and people are **living** things. They need food, water, and air to live and grow. **Nonliving** things do not need food, water, and air.

living

nonliving

Living Things

Flowers and dogs are living things. They need food, water, and air to grow and change. They come from other living things.

■ How do you know the flower is a living thing?

Nonliving Things

A rock and a chair are nonliving things.
They do not need food, water, and air.
They do not grow.

■ **How can you tell these are nonliving things?**

Compare Living and Nonliving Things

How can you tell if something is living?
Ask these questions.

- Does it need food, water, and air?
- Does it grow and change?

If you say yes both times, the thing is living.

■ How are these bears the same?

■ How are they different?

These pictures show living things and nonliving things. Water can move, but it is a nonliving thing. It does not need food and air.

- ■ **Which things in these pictures are living and nonliving?**

Think About It

1. What is a living thing?

2. What is a nonliving thing?

 Health/Career Link

A Doctor Observes People

This doctor is using her senses as she gives the boy a checkup. She listens to his heart. She looks at his throat.

 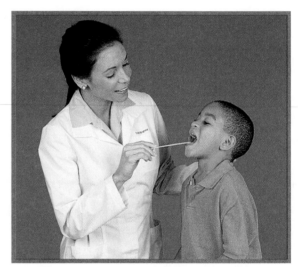

■ **Which sense is the doctor using in each picture?**

Think and Do

Draw a picture of a doctor. Then show your picture. Tell how doctors use their senses in their work.

Measure with a Growth Chart

This girl can tell she is growing. Her mother measures her on a growth chart. She is taller now than she was a year ago.

Mary

September 25

Think and Do

Make a growth chart. Have someone help you mark how tall you are. Write the date. Measure how tall you are each month.

Tell What You Know

1. Which senses would you use to learn more about each thing?

Vocabulary

Tell which pictures go with the words.

2. living thing

3. nonliving thing

a.   **b.**   **c.**   **d.**

Using Science Skills

4. **Observe** Collect things in an egg carton. Use two words to tell how each thing feels, looks, sounds, or smells. Have a partner guess each thing.

5. **Compare** Make a chart to compare a pencil and a plant. Draw pictures of them. Tell if the things are living or nonliving.

Living or Nonliving?			
Thing	Picture	Does it need air and water?	Does it grow?
pencil			
plant			

CHAPTER 2

All About Plants

Vocabulary

roots
stem
leaves
flower
seed
seed coat
sunlight

Did You Know?
The rafflesia is the biggest **flower** in the world.

A20

Did You Know?
There is a plant that has **leaves** that look like elephant ears.

What Are the Parts of a Plant?

Plant Parts

You will need

carrot

plant with flower

paper and pencil

1 Look at the parts of one plant. Draw what you see.

2 Look at the parts of the other plant. Draw what you see.

3 Compare the plants. Tell about their parts.

Science Skill

When you compare things, you tell how they are the same and different.

Parts of a Plant

Plants have different parts. Most plants have roots, a stem, and leaves. Many plants also have flowers.

flower

leaf

stem

roots

How Plant Parts Help a Plant

Plants have many shapes and sizes.
Most plants have the same parts.
These parts help them live and grow.

Roots

The **roots** hold plants in the soil. The roots also take in water.

■ **What part of a carrot do you eat?**

■ **Where are the stems in these pictures?**

Stems

The **stem** helps hold up the plant.
Water moves up the stem to the leaves.

A tree trunk is also a stem. Water
moves up the trunk to the tree's leaves.

Leaves

The **leaves** make food for the plant. Leaves from different plants have different shapes.

■ **What shapes do you see?**

Flowers

Many plants also have flowers.
The **flowers** make seeds.

■ What part of the plant is this bee on?

Think About It

1. How are plants the same?
2. How are they different?

How Do Plants Grow?

The Inside of a Seed

You will need

bean seed

hand lens

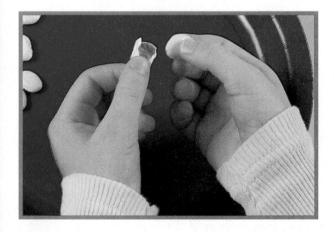

1 Peel off the covering of the seed.

2 Open the seed.

3 Observe. Tell what is inside.

Science Skill

Use a hand lens to help you observe.

How Plants Grow

Most plants grow from a **seed**. The seed may have a covering called a **seed coat**. The seed coat falls away as the plant grows.

leaves

stem

roots

seed

seed coat

Plants Grow from Seeds

Different plants grow from different seeds. The new plants look like the plants the seeds came from. When old plants die, their seeds can be planted to grow new plants.

■ **Observe the seeds. How are they the same and different?**

tomato seeds

sunflower seeds

apple seeds

corn seeds

dandelion seeds

orange seeds

Think About It

1. Where do new plants come from?
2. What will the plant that grows from a seed look like?

What Do Plants Need?

What Plants Need to Grow

You will need

seeds

2 clear cups

any color cup

soil

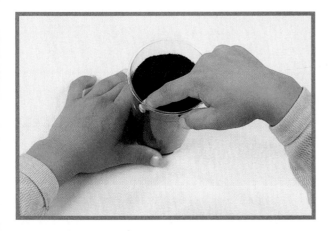

1 Fill one clear cup with soil. Plant two seeds near the side. Water.

2 Put the cup with the seeds into the cup with color. After 3 days, take it out.

3 Share what you see.

Science Skill

When you share your ideas, you communicate with others.

What Plants Need to Live

Plants need four things to live and grow.
What are these four things?

air

light

soil

water

How Plants Grow and Live

Light and Air

A plant's leaves use light and air to make the plant's food. Light from the sun is called **sunlight**.

Water

Plants also need water to grow and stay healthy. Water helps move food to all parts of the plant.

■ How do this plant's leaves help the plant live?

Different kinds of plants grow in different places around the world. All these plants need light, air, and water.

■ **Where is the water in each of these pictures?**

Think About It

1. What do plants need to live and grow?
2. How do leaves use light and air?

Art Link

An Artist Observes Plants

An artist named Vincent van Gogh painted these flowers long ago. Artists look closely at things around them.

- **What parts of a plant can you see in this picture?**

- **What part is missing?**

Sunflowers by Vincent van Gogh

Think and Do

Paint your own picture of a plant. Show at least two parts.

A36

Math Link

Measure a Plant

You can use a ruler to measure how tall a plant grows. You can also use a pencil or a stick if you do not have a ruler.

Think and Do

Watch a plant grow. Put a pencil in the soil next to the plant. Mark how tall the plant is. Every three days, mark how much the plant has grown.

Tell What You Know

1. Tell what you know about each picture.

Vocabulary

Tell which picture goes with each word or words.

2. roots

3. leaves

4. stem

5. flowers

6. sunlight

7. seed

8. seed coat

a. **b.** **c.** **d.**

e. **f.** **g.**

Using Science Skills

9. Compare Roots take in water. Stems help plants stand up. Think about the parts of your body that take in water or help you stand up. How are you the same as a plant? How are you different?

10. Observe Make a chart about leaves where you live.

Find two leaves. Glue or tape them on your chart. Tell about your leaves.

Leaves			
Leaf	Shape	Color	Size

CHAPTER **3**

All About Animals

Vocabulary

gills
mammal
reptile
amphibian
insect
hatch
larva
pupa
tadpoles

Did You Know?
A gecko is a
reptile that can
crawl up trees.

Did You Know?

There are more kinds of beetles than any other kind of insect.

What Do Animals Need?

An Animal Home

You will need

plastic box and gloves

soil, twig, and rocks

water in a bottle cap

small animals

1 Put the soil, twig, rocks, water, and animals in the box.

2 Observe. How does your home give the animals food, water, and a place to hide?

3 Draw what you see. Close the lid.

Science Skill

When you observe the animals in their home, you can see how they meet their needs.

What Animals Need

All animals need food, water, air, and a place to live. These ducks live by a pond. Why is this a good home for them?

mallard ducks

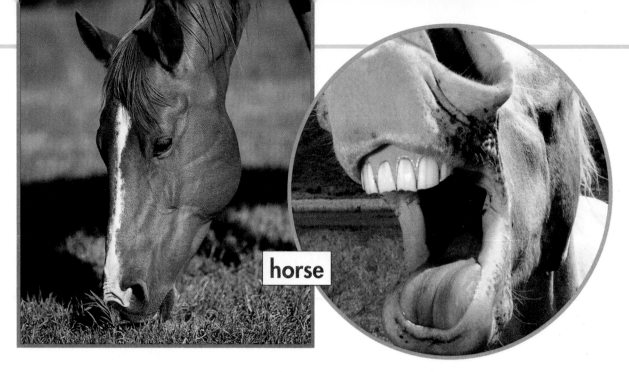

horse

Animals Need Food

Different kinds of animals need different kinds of food to live and grow. Horses eat grass, but lions eat meat. A horse's flat teeth are good for chewing grass. A lion's sharp teeth are good for tearing meat.

■ **What do an animal's teeth tell you about what it eats?**

mountain lion

Animals Need Water

All animals need water to live. Like many animals, a camel drinks with its mouth. It also gets water from the food it eats. An elephant uses its trunk to put water in its mouth.

■ **How are the camels and the elephant getting the water they need?**

camels

elephant

Animals Need a Place To Live

All animals need a place to live.
A bat can find a home in a cave.
A falcon can build a nest.
Animals keep safe and raise their
young in their homes.

bat

peregrine falcons

Park Ranger

Many animals have homes
in parks. If they need help,
park rangers take care of
them.

Animals Need Air

All animals need air to live and grow. Special body parts help them get it. Some animals have a nose and lungs. Others, like this fish, have **gills** that take air from water.

cow

gills

Think About It

1. What do animals need to live and grow?
2. What are some ways animals meet these needs?

What Are Some Kinds of Animals?

Investigate

Animals in Your Neighborhood

You will need

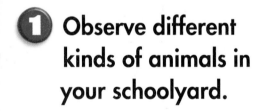

paper and pencil

1 Observe different kinds of animals in your schoolyard.

2 Draw a picture of each animal you observe.

3 Classify the animals into groups. How are the animals in each group the same?

Science Skill

When you classify animals, you observe how they are the same. Then you group them.

Different Kinds of Animals

reptile

Scientists observe how animals are the same and different. They put animals that are the same into groups. Here are some kinds of animals.

birds

mammal

fish

amphibian

Mammals

A **mammal** is an animal that feeds its young milk. A mammal also has hair or fur on its body.

■ How can you tell these animals are mammals?

whitetail deer

pig

squirrel

Birds

Birds are animals that have two wings and two feet. They are the only animals that have feathers. Some birds fly, some birds run, and some swim.

macaw

bluebird

flamingo

■ How are all these birds the same?

Reptiles

A **reptile** is an animal with rough, dry skin. It may have scales or hard plates. Alligators and turtles are reptiles.

alligators

giant tortoise

Amphibians

An **amphibian** is an animal with smooth, wet skin. Frogs, toads, and salamanders are amphibians.

salamander

■ How are amphibians different from reptiles?

Fish

Fish live in water. They have special body parts called gills that help them breathe. Their bodies are covered with scales.

snapper

gills

queen angelfish

■ **How are these fish the same?**

Think About It

1. What are some different kinds of animals?
2. How are the animals in all the groups the same? How are they different?

What Are Insects?

A Model of an Insect

You will need

Styrofoam balls

scissors

toothpicks and chenille sticks

wax paper

1 Choose an insect to make. Insects have three body parts and six legs.

2 Choose materials. Make a model of your insect.

 **CAUTION** Be careful with toothpicks, chenille sticks, and scissors. They are sharp.

3 Compare your model with a picture of a real insect.

Science Skill

When you make a model of an insect, you show parts that a real insect has.

Insects

An **insect** is an animal that has three body parts and six legs. Some insects also have wings.

3 body parts

weevil

More About Insects

Insects lay eggs. A ladybug lays hundreds of eggs at one time.

Insects do not have bones. They have a strong body covering. The covering keeps their soft insides safe.

ladybug

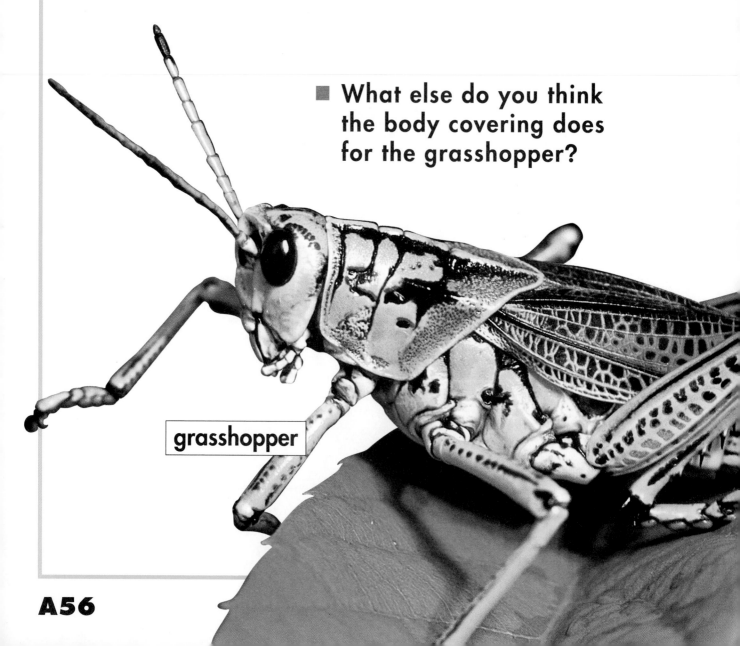

■ **What else do you think the body covering does for the grasshopper?**

grasshopper

A butterfly is an insect. It uses its wings to fly. An ant is an insect, too. Most ants have no wings. They use their legs to move fast.

■ **How are the butterfly and the ant the same and different?**

butterfly

ant

Think About It

1. How can you tell if an animal is an insect?
2. What else do you know about insects?

How Do Animals Grow?

Animals and Their Young

You will need

animal
picture cards

paper and
pencil

Animals and Their Young		
Animal	Same	Different
cats	Both have ears. Both are orange.	One is big. One is small.

1 Match the picture cards. Put each young animal with the adult.

2 Make a chart. Compare the young animal and the adult.

3 Tell how each young animal is like the adult. Tell how it is different.

Science Skill

When you compare the pictures, you tell how they are the same and different.

How Different Kinds of Animals Grow

These young animals will change as they get older. They will grow to look like their parents.

bunny

chick

Ways Animals Begin Life

Rabbits are small when they are born. Their eyes are closed. They can not walk or hop until they are older.

just born

8 days old

■ **How do the chick and the rabbit change in different ways?**

Chicks **hatch**, or break out of eggs. Their eyes are open. Soon they can walk and peck for food.

just hatched

8 days old

8 weeks old

adult

8 weeks old

adult

Animals Care for Their Young

Some animals feed their young. Later they teach them how to find food.

robins

brown bears

■ How do these animals make sure their young have food?

Some animals lick their young to clean them. Later they show them how to clean themselves.

chimpanzees

Some animals stay close to their young to keep them warm. Others keep their young warm in pouches.

- **How do these penguins keep their baby warm?**

emperor penguins

Think About It

1. What are two ways that animals begin life?
2. How do all young animals change as they grow?

How Does a Butterfly Grow?

A Butterfly's Life

You will need

box

caterpillar

paper and pencil

1 Keep your caterpillar in a warm place.

2 Observe your caterpillar every day for three weeks. Draw it each time.

3 How did your caterpillar change? Share what happened.

Science Skill

When you use your senses to observe, you find out how the caterpillar changes.

How a Butterfly Grows

A butterfly is an insect. It hatches from an egg. It changes many times before it grows colorful wings. What do all insects have?

monarch butterfly

From Caterpillar to Butterfly

A butterfly begins life as an egg. A tiny caterpillar, or **larva**, hatches from the egg. The caterpillar eats and grows.

1 egg

2 caterpillar or larva

3 pupa

4 butterfly comes out

Then it stops eating. The caterpillar becomes a **pupa** and makes a hard covering.

Inside the covering, the pupa slowly changes. Finally a butterfly comes out and flies away.

5 adult butterfly

Wings Help Butterflies Keep Safe

Butterfly wings have different shapes and colors. Some wings look like leaves or flowers. These wings help butterflies hide.

Buckeye

Spring Azure

Tiger Swallowtail

Other wings help butterflies trick hungry birds.

■ **How do you think "eye spots" might trick a bird?**

Owl

Dogface

Think About It

1. How does a caterpillar change into a butterfly?
2. What are some ways wings help butterflies keep safe?

How Does a Frog Grow?

A Frog's Life

You will need

picture cards

1 Put the picture cards in sequence. Show how you think a frog changes as it grows.

2 Tell why you put your cards in the order you did.

Science Skill

When you sequence the cards, you show what happens first, next, and last.

How a Frog Grows

A frog is an amphibian. It hatches from an egg. As it grows, it changes many times. When it is an adult, it has long back legs.

leopard frog

From Tadpole to Frog

Frogs lay their eggs in water. Young frogs, or **tadpoles**, hatch from the eggs. They have tails to move and gills to breathe in water. They grow.

■ **How has this tadpole changed?**

3 tadpole with back legs

2 tadpole

1 frog eggs

The tadpoles keep changing. They grow front legs. They get lungs to breathe air. Their tails get smaller. Then they look like little frogs. They climb onto land and grow bigger.

4 tadpole grows front legs, tail gets smaller

5 adult frog

Think About It

1. How does a tadpole change into a frog?
2. What body parts does a tadpole have that a frog does not have?

 Movement/Drama Link

Move Like a Frog

These children think about a time
in a frog's life. Then they
move to show what
that time is like.

 **Think and Do**

Find an open space on the floor.
Show what a frog does as an egg,
a tadpole, or an adult frog.

A74

Find Symmetry

Look at this butterfly's wings. Find the two parts that match. Use your finger to trace a line between the matching parts.

Think and Do

Make a butterfly with wings that match.

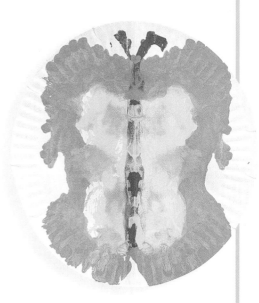

Fold a paper plate in half. Open the plate, and paint patterns on one half. While the paint is wet, press the two halves together. Then open the plate.

How are the two parts the same?

CHAPTER 3 REVIEW

Tell What You Know

1. Tell how these animals are the same. Then tell how they are different.

Vocabulary

Tell which picture goes with each word.

2. mammal

3. reptile

4. amphibian

5. insect

6. gills

7. pupa

8. tadpole

9. hatch

10. larva

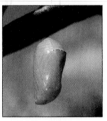 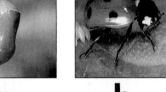

a.　　　**b.**　　　**c.**

d.　　　**e.**　　　**f.**

g.　　　**h.**　　　**i.**

A76

Using Science Skills

11. Classify Make a graph to show groups of animals. Find pictures of animals. Classify your pictures to make a graph like this one.

12. Sequence A butterfly changes as it grows. Write the words in sequence to show how this insect changes.

adult butterfly

larva

egg

pupa

Senses Game

Get a box and put in different things. Ask your family or classmates to close their eyes. Have them use touch and hearing to guess each thing.

Nature Walk

Take a nature walk with your class or with family members. Draw or write about what you observe.

Growing and Changing

Look at photos of yourself with a family member. Talk about how you have changed.

Observe a Pet

With an adult, find a pet to observe. Draw or write about the animal.

What does the pet look like?

What does it eat and drink?

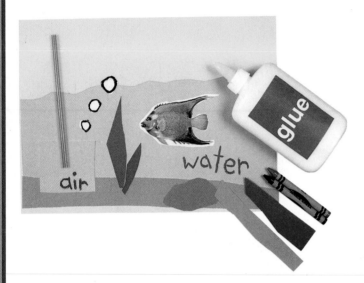

WRITING

Collage What do plants or pets in a classroom need to live? Make a picture. Write your ideas.

READING

The Very Hungry Caterpillar
by Eric Carle
How does the hungry caterpillar use plants? Share your ideas.

COMPUTER CENTER
Visit *The Learning Site* at
www.harcourtschool.com

Living Together

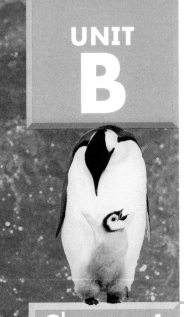

Life Science

Living Together

UNIT PROJECT

Take a Peek!
Find out how plants and animals live in different places. Decorate a box that shows one place.

Plants and Animals Need One Another

Did You Know?
Some animals such as the clownfish use other animals for **shelter**.

How Animals Need Plants

Many animals need plants for food.
Some animals use plants to hide in or to
make nests for their young.

rabbit

carrot top

Animals Need Plants for Food

Some animals eat only plants. Rabbits eat the tops and the roots of carrot plants. Caterpillars eat leaves.

■ **What does this cow eat?**

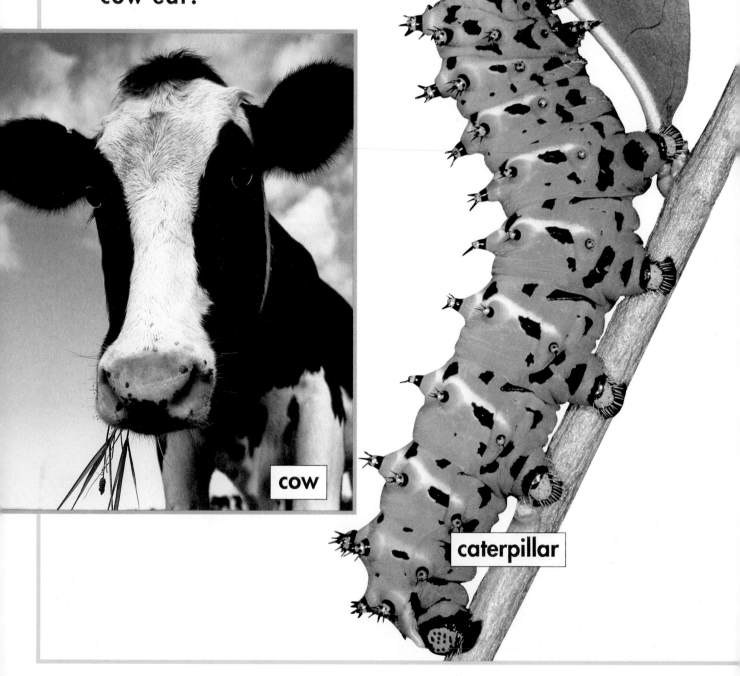

cow

caterpillar

Some animals eat other animals as well as plants. A toucan eats insects as well as fruit. A raccoon eats both fish and berries.

■ **What is this raccoon eating?**

raccoon

toucan

Other Ways Animals Need Plants

Some animals need plants for shelter. A **shelter** is a place where an animal can be safe.

African leopard

■ How does the tree help this leopard keep safe?

Many animals that live in the soil need plants for shelter. They may live inside rotting logs. They eat bits of dead plants.

termites

B8

Some animals make nests with parts of plants. A bird may use grass. An alligator uses leaves and strong reeds.

oriole

deer mice

alligator

■ **What do mice use to make a nest?**

Think About It

1. What are some ways animals need plants?
2. What animals eat only plants? What animals eat other animals as well as plants?

How Do Animals Help Plants?

 Investigate

How Seeds Stick to Animals

You will need

 glue

Styrofoam ball

glue

cotton and other materials to try out

1 Look at this picture. How might these seeds stick to animals?

2 Plan a model of a seed that sticks. Choose materials to glue to the ball.

3 Investigate your materials. Which ones stick to the cotton? The cotton is like animal fur.

Science Skill

To investigate how seeds stick to animals, make a plan to try out different ideas. Follow your plan.

How Animals Help Plants

Some animals carry seeds to new places. Some help make the soil better for plants. Others help flowers make seeds.

Animals Carry Seeds

A seed may stick to a cat's fur. The seed may be carried far from the plant. When the seed falls off, it may grow into a new plant.

seed bur

Animals Help Make Soil Better

earthworm

A worm eats dead plants. Its waste helps **enrich** the soil, or make the soil better for plants.

■ **What things are these animals doing that help plants?**

Animals Help Plants Make Seeds

Flowers have a powder called **pollen** that helps them make seeds. A butterfly carries pollen from flower to flower. The pollen falls off. Those flowers use the pollen to make seeds.

butterfly

Think About It

1. How do small animals make the soil better for plants?
2. How do animals help plants grow new plants?

How Do We Need Plants and Animals?

Things People Use

You will need

picture cards

1 Which pictures show things made from plants? Which are from animals?

2 Classify the cards. Sort them into groups.

3 Share your groups. Tell why each thing belongs.

Science Skill

When you classify the things on the cards, you group them to show ways they are the same.

How People Need Plants and Animals

People need plants and animals for food, clothing, and shelter. Plants and animals also add beauty to people's lives.

What People Need Plants For

People need shelter and clothing. They use plants to make many products. A **product** is something that people make from other things.

cotton shirt

cotton bolls

■ Where did the lumber come from to make this house?

People eat parts of plants. Celery is the stem of a plant. Peanut butter is made from peanuts, the seeds of a plant.

■ **What plant do you like to eat?**

People also use plants to make products they need in their homes.

What People Need Animals For

People use animals for food. Many people eat beef, pork, chicken, and fish. Eggs and milk are also foods from animals.

■ **What parts of this breakfast come from animals? What parts come from plants?**

People use wool from sheep to make clothing. Coats and sweaters may be made with wool.

Guide Dog Trainer

Some people keep animals as pets. Others need animals as helpers. Guide dog trainers work with some dogs. They teach them to help blind people.

Think About It

1. What are some ways people need plants?

2. What are some ways people need animals?

 **Math Link**

Snacks Made from Plants

People make snacks from plants. They mix nuts, dried fruits, and cereal to make a tasty treat. Stores may call this snack *trail mix*.

Think and Do

Make a snack from plants. Measure one cup each of granola, raisins, and nuts into a bowl. Mix them. Eat your trail mix snack.

Keeping a Custom

Long ago, some African Americans in South Carolina made baskets like this one. They wove them from plants. This woman keeps the custom. She weaves a basket as people did long ago.

Think and Do

Paper comes from plants. It is made from the wood of trees. Use strips of colored paper to weave a place mat.

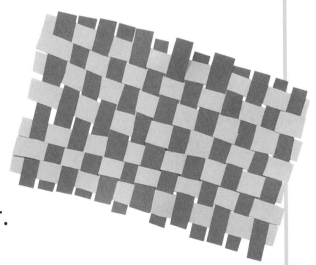

Tell What You Know

1. Tell how animals and people can use these plants to meet their needs.

Vocabulary

Tell which picture goes with each word. Then use the word to tell about the picture.

a.   **b.**

2. enrich

3. shelter

4. pollen

5. product

c.   **d.**

Using Science Skills

6. Classify Collect pictures of different kinds of foods. Put the foods that come from plants in one group. Put the foods that come from animals in another group.

What foods can you find that come from both plants and animals?

7. Observe Make a chart about the ways you use plants and animals. Observe ways you use them at school. Draw pictures in your chart.

Ways I Use Plants and Animals			
	Food	Clothing	Beauty
Plants			
Animals			

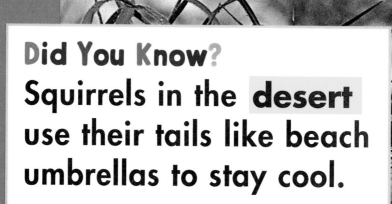

A Place to Live

Vocabulary

forest
desert
rain forest
ocean
algae

Did You Know?
Squirrels in the **desert** use their tails like beach umbrellas to stay cool.

Did You Know?
A plant called **algae** is used to make ice cream.

What Lives in a Forest?

Forest Trees

You will need

dark crayon   pencil and paper

1 Go outside. Find a tree. Draw one of its leaves.

2 Make a rubbing of the tree's bark.

3 Compare your drawing and rubbing with a classmate's.

Science Skill

When you compare drawings and rubbings, look for ways the trees are the same and different.

Forests

A **forest** is a place where many trees grow. A forest floor is shady. The soil stays moist.

forest

Forest Plants and Animals

Some trees grow tall in a forest. Their high leaves catch the sunlight they need to make food.

Berry bushes and mountain laurels need less sunlight than trees. They can grow below the trees.

berry bushes

mountain laurel

Many animals find food and shelter in a forest. Wood thrushes find safe places to build their nests. Box turtles eat worms for food.

wood thrushes

red foxes

■ How are the foxes meeting their needs?

Think About It

1. What is a forest?
2. How do plants and animals in a forest meet their needs?

box turtle

What Lives in the Desert?

Desert Leaves

You will need

2 paper clips   water   wax paper   2 paper-towel leaf shapes

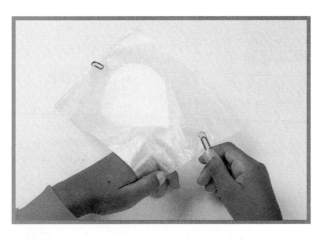

1 Make both leaf shapes damp. Put one shape on wax paper. Fold the paper over. Clip it.

2 Put both leaves in the sunlight. Check them after an hour.

3 Which leaf holds water longer? Draw a conclusion.

Science Skill

To draw a conclusion about desert leaves, think about your leaf with the waxy coat and the other leaf.

Deserts

A **desert** is a dry place. It gets lots of sunlight and little rain. Only a few kinds of plants and animals can live there.

desert

Desert Plants and Animals

Desert plants can hold water to use when they need it. Some, like the yucca, have thick leaves with a waxy coat. Others hold water in their thick stems.

cactus wren

yucca

beavertail cactus

Most deserts are hot. Desert animals have ways to stay cool and get water. Some, like the armadillo, stay in the shade. They look for food at night when it is cooler. Others, like the kangaroo rat, get water from their food.

■ **How do many of these animals stay cool?**

armadillo

rattlesnake

kangaroo rat

Think About It

1. What is a desert?
2. How do plants and animals live in a desert?

What Lives in a Rain Forest?

Rain Forest Plants

You will need

seeds

2 wet cotton balls

film cans and lid with hole

plastic and rubber band

wet cotton ball

seeds

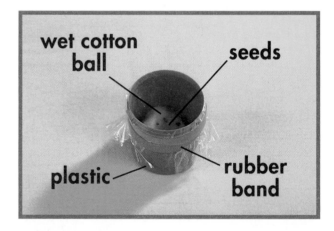

wet cotton ball

seeds

plastic

rubber band

1 Rain forest plants get little light. Make a model of a rain forest like this one. Close lid.

2 Plants in open areas get more light. Make a model of an open area.

3 Set both models in the sun for 5 days. Tell how the cotton changes.

Science Skill

To communicate how the forests grew, draw and share pictures of what you observed.

Rain Forests

A **rain forest** is wet all year. Most rain forests are warm, too. Rain and warm weather help trees and other plants grow. Animals use the plants to meet their needs.

rain forest

Rain Forest Animals and Plants

Animals live at different levels of the rain forest. Macaws live near the treetops. They find fruit to eat. Sloths hang from the middle of trees. They find shelter there and plants to eat.

macaw

three-toed sloths

orchid

Rain forest plants also live at different levels. Most grow from roots in the soil. Some, like the orchid, grow from roots halfway up trees. They get the light they need there.

bromeliad

■ Where does the rain forest plant called a bromeliad live?

Think About It

1. What is a rain forest?
2. How do plants and animals live in a rain forest?

What Lives in the Ocean?

Ocean Animals

You will need

ocean picture cards

1 Which ocean pictures show fish? Which show other animals?

2 Classify the animals. Put them in groups.

3 Share your groups. Talk about other ways to classify the animals.

Science Skill

When you classify the animals, you group them to show ways they are the same.

Oceans

An **ocean** is a large, deep body of salt water. Oceans cover three fourths of the Earth.

ocean

Ocean Plants and Animals

Some ocean plants are called **algae**. Many ocean animals use algae for food and shelter.

parrot fish

■ **What is the parrot fish using the algae for?**

bottle-nosed dolphin

B40

green sea turtle

starfish

Ocean animals can find what they need in ocean waters. Dolphins' strong tails help them swim fast to catch fish.

Sea turtles use their flippers to swim and catch food.

■ How do you think a starfish's shape helps it get food?

Think About It

1. What is an ocean?
2. How do ocean animals get what they need to live?

Math Link

Observe Leaf Patterns

You can find leaf patterns on a tree twig. A tree grows leaves the same way again and again. The leaves make a pattern.

Think and Do

Look at a tree twig with leaves. Observe how the leaves grow in a pattern. Draw a picture that shows the pattern.

A Scientist Investigates the Ocean

Sylvia Earle is a marine biologist, a scientist who studies life in the ocean. She dives deep to find out about ocean plants and animals. She also helps people learn about the ocean.

Think and Do

Choose a plant or an animal that lives in the ocean. Read books to learn more about it. Make a poster that tells about the plant or animal.

Tell What You Know

1. Tell about where each animal lives.

Vocabulary

Tell which picture goes with the word or words.

2. algae

3. rain forest

4. ocean

5. desert

6. forest

a.   **b.**   **c.**

d.   **e.**

Using Science Skills

7. Classify Read the clues. Name each plant or animal. Tell where it lives.

  a. This plant has thorns that keep animals from eating it. It has a waxy coat to keep water in.

  b. This animal has fins for swimming. It uses algae for food and shelter.

  c. This plant lives halfway up on trees. It needs a warm, wet place.

8. Compare Look at the graph. Tell which place gets the most rain in a month.

How Much Rain Falls in a Month?	
Temperate Forest	◊ ◊ ◊ ◊ ◊
Rain Forest	◊ ◊ ◊ ◊ ◊ ◊ ◊ ◊ ◊ ◊ ◊ ◊ ◊ ◊ ◊
Desert	◊

Each ◊ equals 2 centimeters.

What Do Worms Need?

1. Put two kinds of soil and two worms in a covered box.

2. In two hours, check where the worms are.

3. What do the worms need? Talk about what you observe.

Make a Bird Feeder

1. Spread peanut butter on a pinecone.

2. Roll the pinecone in birdseed.

3. Hang the pinecone with string outdoors.

4. Observe birds that eat the seeds.

Rain Forest in a Jar

1. Put pebbles, soil, and plants in a jar.

2. Water the plants. Put the lid on the jar.

3. Put the jar where it gets light but not strong sun.

4. Wait one day. Observe. How is this like a rain forest?

Stems That Store Water

1. Observe the stem pipes, or small dots on a cut celery stalk.

2. Set the stalk in an empty cup. Put it in the sun until it droops.

3. Add water to the cup. Put it in the refrigerator. The next day, tell what happened and why.

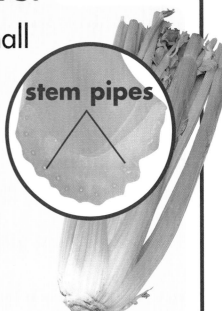

stem pipes

WRITING

Pop-Up Card Fold a sheet of paper. On the outside, write a question about a place. Inside, give a pop-up answer!

READING

All Night Near the Water
by Jim Arnosky

How do ducks and other animals use a lake for shelter and food? Talk about what you find out.

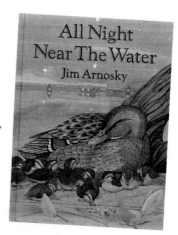

COMPUTER CENTER
Visit *The Learning Site* at
www.harcourtschool.com

About Our Earth

About Our Earth

UNIT PROJECT

On Land and Sea
Make a mural. Show land, air, water, and how people use these things.

Earth's Land

Vocabulary

sand

rock

soil

texture

Did You Know?
Centipedes have
up to 100 pairs of
legs that help them
grip the **soil**.

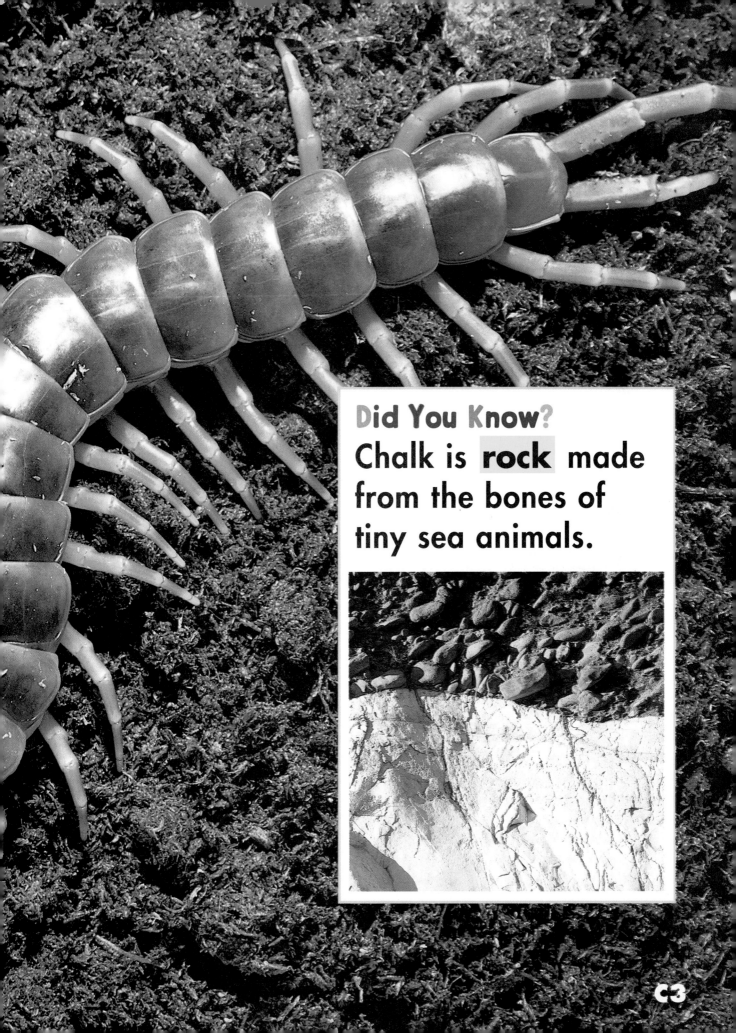

Did You Know?
Chalk is **rock** made
from the bones of
tiny sea animals.

What Can We Observe About Rocks?

Ways to Classify Rocks

You will need

hand lens

different rocks

paper and pencil

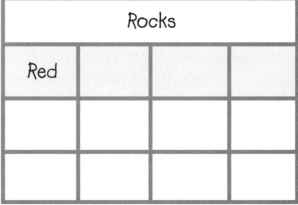

Rocks			
Red			

1 Observe each rock with the hand lens. Feel each rock. Write how the rocks look and feel.

2 Make a chart. Classify your rocks on the chart.

Science Skill

When you classify your rocks, you group them by ways they are the same.

Rocks

A **rock** is a hard, nonliving thing that comes from the Earth. There are many kinds of rocks. People use rocks in different ways.

Different Kinds of Rocks

Some rocks are big, and some are small. Tiny broken pieces of rock are called **sand**. Rocks may be different colors. Some rocks are smooth. Others are rough.

sand

rose quartzite

lava

obsidian

marble

limestone

■ How are these rocks the same? How are they different?

People use rocks to build homes and walls. They melt sand to make glass.

■ **How have these people used rocks?**

Think About It

1. What are rocks?
2. What ways do people use rocks?

What Is Soil?

 Investigate

Observing Soil

You will need

soil

paper plate

hand lens

paper and pencil

Soil		
Looks	Smells	Feels

1 Make a chart like this one. Then observe the soil with a hand lens. Move the soil around.

2 Smell and feel the soil. Think of words that tell about it.

3 Draw pictures and write words that tell about the soil.

Science Skill

When you observe the soil, use your senses to find out how it looks, smells, and feels.

Soil

The Earth's **soil** is made of tiny rocks. It has bits of dead plants and animals in it. Soil has air and water in it too.

All Living Things Use Soil

Plants need soil to grow. Soil has water that plants need. Small pieces of dead plants and animals in soil enrich it.

soybeans

adobe house

People use soil in different ways. Farmers use soil for growing foods. Builders mix soil, water, and straw to make bricks.

Some worms and insects live in soil. Many other animals use soil to make shelters.

■ How do you think this insect uses soil?

Think About It

1. What is soil made of?
2. What are some ways plants and animals use soil?

How Do Different Soils Compare?

How Soils Compare

You will need

hand lens

3 kinds of soil

paper plate

spoon

1 Observe each kind of soil. How does it smell and feel?

2 Put some of each soil on the plate. Use the hand lens to observe.

3 Compare the three kinds of soil. Tell your classmates about them.

Science Skill

When you compare the soils, you tell how they are the same and different.

Different Soils

There are different soils. Each has a different mix of rocks and plants and animal bits. The **texture** of the soil is how it feels.

topsoil

clay soil

sandy soil

How Soils Are Different

Topsoil is dark brown. It has many bits of dead plants and animals in it. Topsoil clumps when it is squeezed. It can hold water.

topsoil

Clay soil may be yellow, red, or brown. It feels sticky, and it clumps when it is squeezed. Clay soil can hold a lot of water.

clay soil

Sandy soil is often light brown. The sand in it makes it feel rough. It does not clump much when it is squeezed. It also does not hold water well.

sandy soil

Think About It

1. What are some different kinds of soil?
2. What are some ways soils are different?

A Geologist Observes Rocks

Florence Bascom was the first American woman to become a geologist. A geologist is a person who studies rocks.

In summer Florence Bascom collected rocks. In winter she studied and wrote about them.

Think and Do

Collect some rocks. Read books to find out about them. Then make a display that tells others what you learned.

Measure Mass

Long ago, people used rocks to measure mass. They put an object on one side of a balance. They added rocks to the other side until the two sides balanced. The number of rocks told the mass of the object.

Your baby weighs 2 stones.

Think and Do

Collect some rocks that are about the same size. Use a balance to measure the mass of some objects.

REVIEW

Tell What You Know

1. Look at the pictures. Tell what you know about each kind of soil.

Vocabulary

Tell which picture goes with each word.

2. sand

3. rock

4. soil

5. texture

a.

b.

c.

d.

Using Science Skills

6. **Classify** Find two kinds of soil where you live. Put each kind in a small bag. Then make a chart like this one. Tape the bags to your chart. Label each bag *topsoil, clay soil,* or *sandy soil.*

Kinds of Soil Where I Live			
Kind of Soil	Color	How It Feels	How It Smells
topsoil			
clay soil			

7. **Compare** Scientists compare how hard rocks are. You can, too. Find different rocks. Use a nail to scratch each one. Soft rocks scratch easily. The hardest rocks won't scratch at all.

Which rock is the hardest? Which is the softest? Tell how you know.

CHAPTER 2

Earth's Air and Water

Did You Know?
The largest **lake**
in the world is in
North America.

Did You Know?
You can move **air** from one container to another underwater.

Where Is Air on Earth?

 Investigate

Air in a Bag

You will need

plastic bag

1 Pull an open bag toward you. Then hold the top of the bag closed.

2 Squeeze the bag. What do you observe? Poke a hole in the bag.

3 What was in the bag? How did you infer that?

Science Skill

When you infer, you use what you observe and know to make a good guess.

Where Air Is

Air is something that people can not see, taste, or smell. Yet air is all around.

■ **What is lifting up the kite in this picture?**

Air Is All Around

You can not see air, but you can see what it does. Air can blow the leaves of trees.

You can feel air when it blows on your skin. You can feel air move through your nose and into your body.

■ **How do you know air is in these pictures?**

Air is in the soil under your feet. It is also in the water you drink.

Air is in the streams, rivers, lakes, and oceans of the Earth. Most of the plants and animals of the Earth need air to live.

Think About It

1. How do you know where air is?
2. Where is air?

Where Is Fresh Water Found?

Investigate

Making Salt Water Fresh

You will need

rubber band

salt, bucket, and sand

marbles and plastic wrap

2 cups and water

1 Mix some salt in water. Taste the water. Pour the water into the bucket. Throw away used cups.

2 Put another cup in the bottom of the bucket. Cover. Put marbles on top.

3 Place the bucket in the sun. Wait two hours. Take the cup out. Taste the water. Draw a conclusion.

Science Skill

To draw a conclusion, think about what you observed and what you know about water.

Fresh Water

Water that is not salty is called **fresh water**. Rain is fresh water. Rain makes puddles or sinks into the ground.

Where Fresh Water Comes From

Rain and melted snow run down mountains. They may form a **stream**, a small body of moving water.

The stream may flow into a **river**, a larger body of moving water. The river flows into a lake. A **lake** is a body of water with land all around it.

stream

river

lake

People need fresh water for drinking, cooking, and washing.

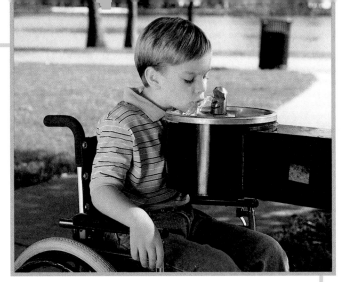

Water Testers

Water from lakes and rivers is cleaned. Then people can drink it. A water tester checks water. The clean water flows through pipes to people's homes.

Think About It

1. What is fresh water?
2. Where do we find fresh water?

Where Is Salt Water on Earth?

 Investigate

Salt and Salt Water

You will need

 hand lens

 salt and spoon

 cup of water

 plate

1 Observe salt on a plate. Draw or write about it.

2 Stir the salt into the water until you can not see it. Write about it.

3 Put some salt water on the plate. Leave it all night. Then communicate what is left on the plate.

Science Skill

When you communicate, use your writing to help you tell others what you observed.

Salt Water

Water that has salt in it is called **salt water**. Salt water tastes and smells salty. The water in the oceans is salt water.

Where Salt Water Is

Salt water is in oceans which cover most of the Earth. Salt water is also in some rivers that flow into oceans. A few lakes have salt water, too.

■ **What part of the Earth looks blue from space?**

How Salt Water Is Used

In some places, people take the salt out of ocean water. Then they have fresh water to use. They may use the salt on their food.

Think About It

1. What is salt water?
2. Where is the Earth's salt water?

 **Literature Link**

The Puddle
by David McPhail

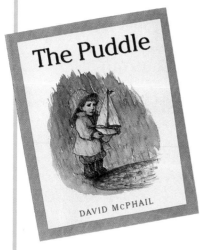

In this book, a boy starts to sail his boat in a puddle. Then some animal friends come by and everything changes.

Have someone share *The Puddle* with you. Find out how the boy and his friends use the puddle. See what happens when the sun comes out.

Think and Do

Make a puddle on a plastic plate. Use a crayon to draw around it. Let the sun shine on your puddle. Observe what happens.

How Much of the Earth Is Ocean?

Oceans cover most of the Earth. In fact, oceans cover three fourths of it.

Think and Do

Use a paper plate to show how much of the Earth oceans cover.

1. Fold a paper plate in half.

2. Fold the plate in half again the other way. You will have four parts called fourths.

3. Color three of the fourths blue.

4. Color one fourth brown.

Tell What You Know

1. Tell what you know about each picture.

Vocabulary

Tell which picture goes with the word or words.

2. air

3. fresh water

4. stream

5. river

6. lake

7. salt water

a.   b.   c.

d.   e.   f.

Using Science Skills

8. Infer Hold a cup upside down. Push it under the water. Then tip it to one side. Observe. Infer what was in the cup.

9. Communicate Get a cup of fresh water and a cup of salt water. Put a few drops of each kind on ice. What happens?

Make a chart. Tell how fresh water is different from salt water. Communicate to classmates what you find out.

Fresh Water and Salt Water Are Different		
	Fresh Water	Salt Water
How Does It Look?		
How Does It Taste?		
What Does It Do to Ice?		

Observe Soil Layers

1. Put soil in a jar.
2. Fill the jar with water.
3. Put the lid on tight. Shake.
4. Wait for the soil to settle.
   Draw what you observe.

Make a Soil Key

1. Fold an index card into four parts. Cut a hole in the middle.
2. Color each part black, brown, yellow-orange, or orange-brown.
3. Put the card on top of some soil near your home. Which color matches?
4. Brown and black soils are good for growing plants. Tell about your soil.

How Much Air Is In a Breath?

1. Take a big breath.

2. Let it out by blowing into a balloon.

3. With your fingers, hold the end of the balloon closed. Observe how much air you breathed out.

4. Compare balloon breaths to a classmate's or family member's.

Visit a Shoreline

1. With your class or family members, visit a shoreline.

2. Observe the soil. Dig at it.

3. Draw pictures of any shells, rocks, plants, or animals you observe.

4. Share your drawings.

WRITING

Earth Book Make a book in the shape of Earth. On each page, tell one way people use air, water, rocks, or soil.

READING

Water
by Frank Asch
Where is water on Earth? How is it used? Read and share your ideas.

COMPUTER CENTER
Visit **The Learning Site** at www.harcourtschool.com

Weather and the Seasons

Earth Science

Weather and the Seasons

UNIT PROJECT

The Four Seasons

Make a mobile for each season. Show plants, animals, weather, and clothing.

CHAPTER

1

Measuring Weather

Vocabulary

weather
temperature
thermometer
wind
water vapor
evaporate
condense
water cycle

Did You Know?
You don't have to
have rainy **weather**
to get lightning.

D2

Did You Know?
A landsailer can go more than 100 miles an hour in the **wind** .

What Is Weather?

 Investigate

Weather Conditions

You will need

paper

markers

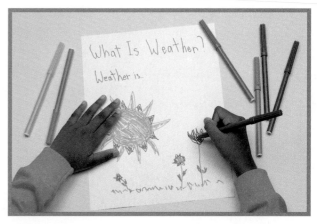

1 Observe the changes in weather.

2 Draw or write what you observe.

3 Compare observations with a classmate. Add your page to a class book.

Science Skill

When you compare the things you observed, tell how they are the same and different.

Weather

It may be hot or cold outside. It may be sunny, cloudy, or rainy. All these words tell about weather. The **weather** is what the air outside is like.

rainy weather

Different Kinds of Weather

When the air outside changes, the weather changes. The weather may be hot one day and cool the next.

One day may be cloudy and rainy. The next day may be clear and sunny. One day may be very windy. Another day may be calm.

■ **How are these kinds of weather different?**

Meteorologist

People like to know what the weather will be. They check weather reports made by a meteorologist. A meteorologist is a scientist who studies weather.

Think About It

1. What is weather?
2. How can weather change from day to day?

What Is Temperature?

Investigate

Measuring Air Temperature

You will need

thermometer   paper and pencil   red crayon

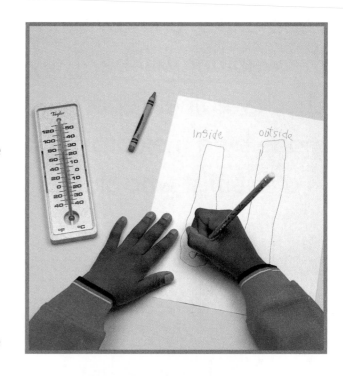

1 Draw and label two thermometers.

2 Measure and record the air temperature in the classroom.

3 Put the thermometer outside for 5 minutes. Measure and record the air temperature.

4 Compare the temperatures.

Science Skill

To measure temperature with a thermometer, read the number next to the top of the red line.

Temperature

The **temperature** is the measure of how hot or cold something is. Temperature is measured with a tool called a **thermometer**.

thermometer

■ **What is the temperature on the thermometer?**

D9

Different Temperatures

The temperature of the air changes from day to day. It also changes as the seasons change. Sometimes it is so low that water freezes. Sometimes it is so high that an ice pop melts.

■ **How does the temperature change in these pictures?**

Air temperature may also change during the day. In the daytime the sun warms the air. The temperature goes up.

At night the sun does not warm the air. The temperature goes down, and the air feels cooler.

daytime

early evening

■ **How are the temperatures different here? Why?**

Think About It

1. What is a thermometer? How do you use it?

2. What is temperature? How does it change?

What Is Wind?

 Investigate

Wind Direction

You will need

drinking straw

round toothpick

paper triangle

tape

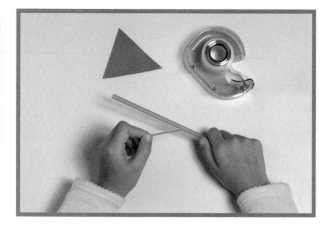

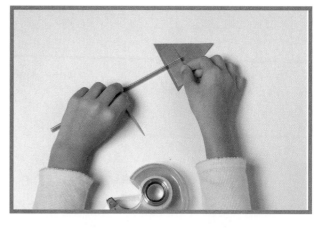

1 Make a wind vane. Poke the toothpick through the straw.

CAUTION Be careful. Toothpicks are sharp.

2 Tape the triangle to the straw. Go outdoors. Hold up the toothpick.

3 Observe the wind's direction on two windy days.

Science Skill

To observe the wind's direction, check which way the triangle points.

Wind

Moving air is called **wind**. Wind can push things. It can push a sailboat across a lake or blow a wind vane.

wind vane

N 2695

N·4139

Different Kinds of Wind

Sometimes the wind blows gently. Sometimes it blows hard.

A flag can show how hard the wind is blowing. When the wind blows gently, a flag ripples. When it blows hard, a flag flies straight out.

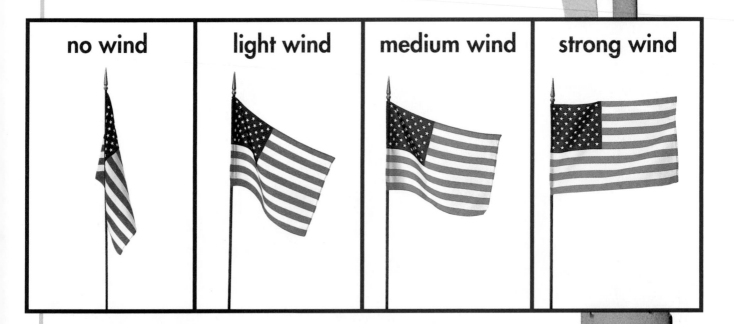

| no wind | light wind | medium wind | strong wind |

■ **How does a flag show how hard the wind is blowing?**

Strong wind turns windmills to make electricity. Sometimes wind can be too strong. The strong winds of a tornado can break up buildings.

Think About It

1. What is wind?
2. What are some different kinds of wind?

What Makes Clouds and Rain?

Investigate

How Clouds Form

You will need

jar with lid

very warm water

ice cubes

1 Pour warm water into the jar. Wait. Pour out most of the water.

CAUTION Be careful. Water is hot!

2 Set the lid upside down on the jar. Observe the jar.

3 Put ice on the lid. Observe. Infer how clouds form.

Science Skill

To infer, first observe. Then think about what happened and draw a conclusion.

Clouds and Rain

Clouds are made up of many tiny drops of water. The drops may join and get heavier. When the drops get too heavy, they fall as rain.

The Water Cycle

Water moves from the Earth to the sky and back again in the **water cycle**.

2 Water vapor meets cooler air. It will then **condense**, or change into tiny drops of water. The drops form clouds.

1 The sun warms water and air. The water will **evaporate**, or change into water vapor.

Water vapor is water that you can not see in the air.

3 The water drops join and get heavier. They fall to Earth as rain, hail, sleet, or snow.

Think About It

1. How do clouds form?
2. How does rain form?

Math Link

Measure Air Temperature

Monday

Tuesday

In some places the air temperature changes a lot from day to day. In other places it changes only a little.

Temperature Changes	
Day of Week	Degrees Fahrenheit
Monday	60
Tuesday	40
Wednesday	

Think and Do

Use a thermometer. Measure and record the temperature each day. Tell about the temperature changes.

Weather Sayings

Long ago, sailors looked for patterns to predict the weather. This is one of their sayings.

<u>Red sky</u> at night,
Sailors' delight.
<u>Red sky</u> at morning,
Sailors take warning.

Sailors observed that a red sunset often comes before a sunny day. A red sunrise often comes before a rainy day.

Think and Do

Observe the weather for a week. Look for patterns. Make up a weather saying about a pattern you observe.

Tell What You Know

1. Tell what you know about the diagram. Use the words *water cycle, water vapor, evaporate,* and *condense.*

Vocabulary

Use each word to tell about the picture.

2.
weather

3.
temperature

4.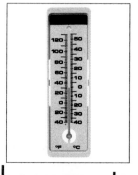
thermometer

5.
wind

Using Science Skills

6. Compare Make a chart about the weather. Observe and compare the weather in the morning and in the afternoon. Tell about the changes.

Today's Weather		
	Morning	Afternoon
How It Looks		
How It Sounds		
How It Feels		
How It Smells		

7. Observe Collect or draw pictures of clouds. Write a label for each picture.

Write a sentence that tells what each cloud looks like. Tell what weather you might have with that cloud.

The Seasons

Vocabulary

season

spring

summer

fall

winter

Did You Know?
Many parts of the world have four seasons, but the tropical rain forest only has one **season**.

Did You Know?
When it is **summer** in North America, it is **winter** in South America.

D25

What Is Spring?

What Helps Seeds Sprout

You will need

4 bean seeds

2 cups

mist bottle

paper towels

hand lens

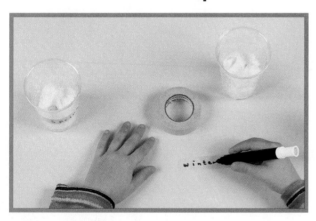

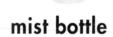

1 Put a damp paper towel in each cup. Add two seeds to each. Label the cups *winter* and *spring*.

2 Put the *winter* cup in a cold, dark place. Put the *spring* cup in a warm, dark place.

3 Observe the seeds with the hand lens three days later. What can you infer?

Science Skill

To infer, first observe, and then think about what you see.

Spring

A **season** is a time of year. **Spring** is the season that follows winter. In spring, there are more hours of daylight. The air gets warmer. Spring rains fall.

spring summer fall winter

Plants and Animals in Spring

More daylight, warmer air, and spring rains help plants start growing. For farmers, spring is a good time to plant seeds.

■ How does spring help these plants start growing?

■ **Which are the young animals?**

Many animals give birth to their young in spring. Birds build nests and lay eggs. Lambs and other animals are born. The growing plants are food for many young animals.

Think About It

1. What is a season?

2. What is spring?

What Is Summer?

Colors That Can Keep You Cool

You will need

4 thermometers

4 colors of paper

stapler

clock

1 Fold and staple 4 color sheets of paper to make sleeves. Put a thermometer in each. Place in the sun.

2 Record the starting temperatures for each.

3 Wait 30 minutes. Record the temperatures again. Order from hottest to coolest.

Science Skill

To put the colors in order, start with the one with the hottest temperature. End with the coolest.

Summer

Summer is the season that follows spring. Summer has the most hours of daylight of any season. In many places the air gets hot.

spring summer fall winter

Plants and Animals in Summer

In summer, lots of sunlight helps plants grow leaves and flowers. Soon fruits begin to form and grow.

■ **What do these plants get in summer that helps them make fruit?**

In summer, young animals eat and grow. Young horses, called foals, become strong and fast.

Young birds lose their first feathers. They begin to look like adults.

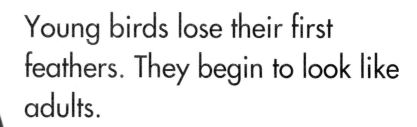

Think About It

1. What is summer?
2. How is summer different from spring?

What Is Fall?

Storing Apples

You will need

apple rings

string

plastic bag

paper and pencil

1 Put some apple rings in the plastic bag. Store them on a shelf.

2 Hang the other apple rings on string. Don't let them touch.

3 Predict and record what will happen.

4 Wait one week. Record.

Science Skill

To predict which way to store apple rings is better, use what you know about food. Then decide.

Fall

The season that follows summer is **fall**. In fall, there are fewer hours of daylight. The air grows cool. In some places, leaves change colors and drop to the ground.

spring   summer   fall   winter

Plants and Animals in Fall

In fall, plants get less sunlight and stop growing bigger. They make seeds that will sprout next spring. Fruits and vegetables are ready to be picked.

■ **What made these plants stop growing bigger?**

When plants stop growing, animals have less food. Some animals move to places where there is more food. Others store food so they have something to eat in winter.

Think About It

1. What is fall?
2. How is fall different from summer?

What Is Winter?

Keeping Warm in Cold Weather

You will need

plastic bag

container of
ice water

things to keep
your hand warm

1 Put your hand in the bag. Then put your hand in the ice water. Does the bag keep your hand warm?

2 What could you put in the bag to keep your hand warm? Choose some things to try.

3 Investigate your ideas by trying them. Which one works best?

Science Skill

To investigate how to keep your hand warm, try out each of your ideas.

Winter

Winter is the season that follows fall. There are fewer hours of daylight than in fall. In many places the air gets cold and snow falls.

spring   summer   fall   winter

Plants and Animals in Winter

In winter, days do not have many hours of sunlight. The branches of many trees and bushes are bare.

Some plants are resting. Some plants that made seeds are now dead.

Where winters are cold, animals can not find much food. Some eat food they stored in fall.

■ How do these animals meet their needs for food in winter?

Think About It

1. What is winter?
2. What are some ways animals live in winter?

 Art Link

A Photographer Observes the Seasons

Ansel Adams was a photographer. Each season, he took pictures of his favorite places. His photographs help us see the beauty of the seasons.

fall

winter

Think and Do

Think of your favorite place. Draw pictures to show it in different seasons. Label each picture with the season it shows.

Read a Graph

In a part of northern California, some seasons are wet and some are dry. This graph shows about how many inches of rain fall in each season.

How Many Inches of Rain?											
Winter											
Spring											
Summer											
Fall											
	1	2	3	4	5	6	7	8	9	10	11

Think and Do

Look at the bar graph. Which season is the wettest in northern California? Which is the driest?

Tell What You Know

1. Tell what you know about the pictures. Use the word *spring*, *summer*, *fall*, or *winter* to tell about each one.

Vocabulary

Use each word to tell about the picture.

2.

season

3.

spring

4.

summer

5.

fall

6.

winter

Using Science Skills

7. **Order** Use four sheets of paper. On each, write the name of one of the seasons. Then draw the clothes you would wear. Put your sheets in order, beginning with summer.

8. **Predict and Investigate** Look at the colors of these shirts. Predict which color will stay the coolest in hot sun. Write your prediction. Use any color paper to investigate your idea.

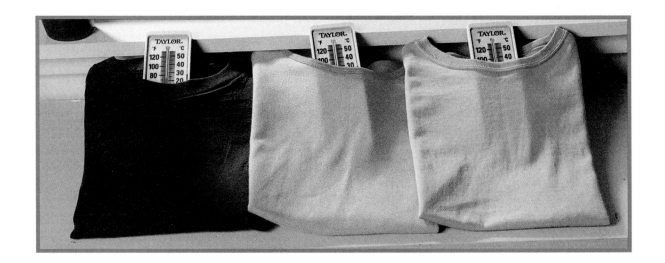

Make a Sail for a Car

Put a paper sail on a toy car. Blow on the sail to make the car move. What could you do to make a better sail? Try your ideas.

Investigate Water Vapor

1. With an adult present, blow into a small plastic bag.

2. Observe the water drops inside. They come from the water vapor in your breath.

3. Put the bag in a freezer for five minutes. Tell what happens.

4. Put the bag in the sun for five minutes. Tell what happens.

Make a Four Seasons Poster

Fold a big sheet of paper into four parts. Label each part for a different season. Add pictures of things you like to do in each season. Talk about your poster.

Find Seasons in a Closet

What clothes do people wear at different times of the year where you live? Brainstorm ideas. Write a list that shows at least two things for each season.

WRITING

Flap Facts Make a flap book about the seasons. Under each flap, tell one thing about that season.

READING

Animal Seasons
by Brian Wildsmith
Read about ways plants and animals change with the seasons. Talk about how the weather changes.

COMPUTER CENTER
Visit *The Learning Site* at
www.harcourtschool.com

Matter and
Energy

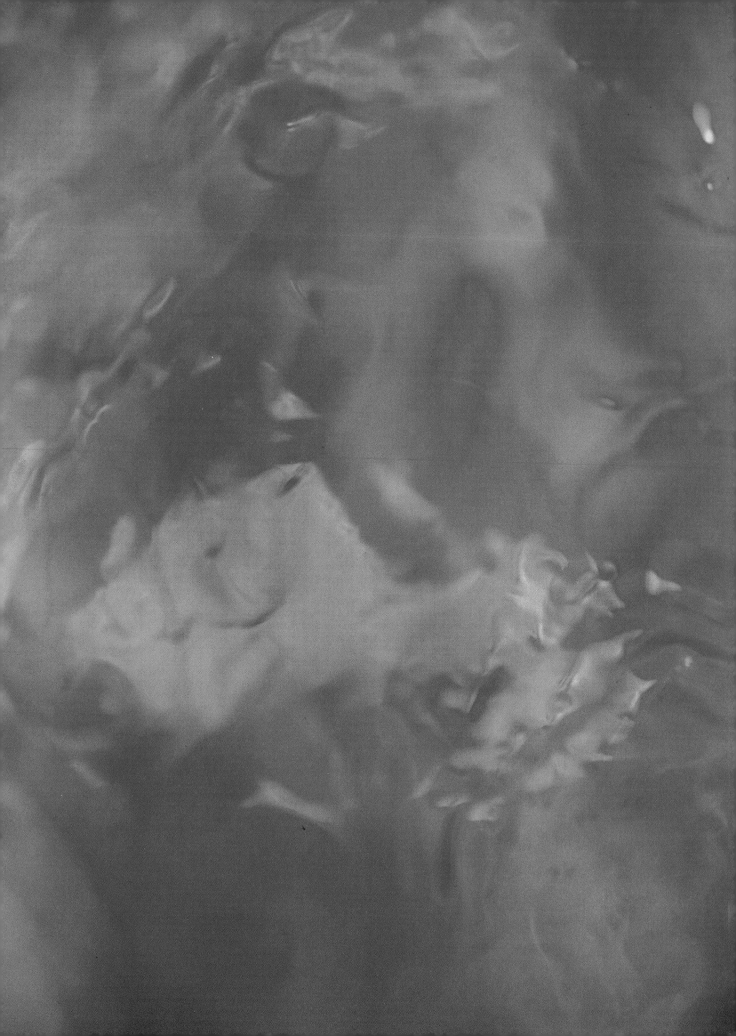

Matter and Energy

UNIT PROJECT

Show Time!

Practice making shadow puppets. Give a puppet show about heat and light.

Investigate Matter

Vocabulary

solid
matter
liquid
float
sink
gas
change
mechanic

Did You Know?
Boats **float** higher
in salt water than
they do in fresh water.

What Can We Observe About Solids?

Solid Objects

You will need

objects

paper and pencil

1 Observe each object.

2 Compare the sizes, shapes, and colors of the objects.

3 Think of three ways to classify the objects. Draw or write them on your paper.

Science Skill

To classify the objects, find ways they are the same and group them.

E4

Matter and Solids

Everything around you is **matter**.
Toys and blocks are matter. You are, too!

■ **What matter do you see?**

Observing Solids

Some matter is solid. A **solid** is matter that keeps its shape. It keeps its shape even when you move it.

■ **How do you know these toys are solids?**

Sorting Solids

You can sort solids in many ways. You can sort toys by color. This graph shows how many toys of each color there are.

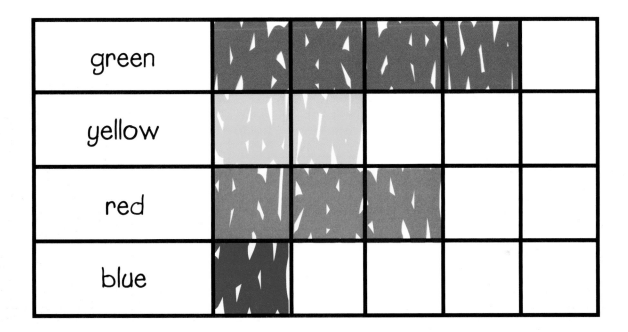

green					
yellow					
red					
blue					

■ **What other ways could you sort the toys in the toy box?**

Think About It

1. What is matter?

2. What is a solid?

What Can We Observe About Liquids?

Investigate

Liquids in Bottles

You will need

3 containers

measuring cup

paper and pencil

1 Draw the shape of the water in each container.

2 Which container do you think has the most water?

3 Measure the water. Write a number for each container. Use the numbers to tell what you found out.

Science Skill

You can write numbers when you measure. Use the numbers to compare the things you measured.

Liquids

Matter that flows is called a **liquid**. A liquid does not have a shape of its own. It takes the shape of the container you pour it into.

Observing Liquids

Some liquids, like water, are thin. Others are thick. Some liquids mix with water. Some, such as oil, do not mix with water.

Thin liquids flow quickly.
Thick liquids flow slowly.
This pan has dish soap,
honey, and juice
running down it.

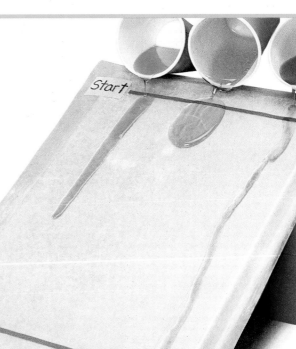

Which Liquid Flows Fastest?	
Liquid	Time
dish soap	9 seconds
honey	47 seconds
juice	1 second

■ **Read the chart. Which liquid flows fastest?**

Think About It

1. What is a liquid?

2. What can we observe about liquids?

What Objects Sink or Float?

Shapes That Sink or Float

You will need

ball of clay

aquarium with water

paper and pencil

1 Gather data about shapes that sink or float. Put the clay ball in the water.

2 Record data about what happens.

3 Make the clay into different shapes. Do they sink or float? Record.

Science Skill

When you gather data, you observe things. When you record data, you write and draw what you observe.

Objects That Sink or Float

Some objects **float** , or stay on top of a liquid. Others **sink** , or drop to the bottom of a liquid. You can change the shape of some objects to make them float or sink.

Floaters and Sinkers

Some objects have shapes that help them float. Others have shapes that make them sink.

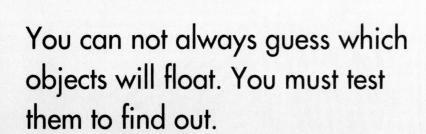

You can not always guess which objects will float. You must test them to find out.

You can group objects as floaters or sinkers. What objects here would you put into these two groups? Why?

Think About It

1. What do *float* and *sink* mean?
2. What helps an object sink or float?

What Can We Observe About Gases?

 **Investigate**

Air in a Bottle

You will need

balloon

plastic soft drink bottle

1 Squeeze the bottle to observe the air in it. Blow up the balloon. Feel the air come out.

2 Put the balloon in the bottle. Pull the end over the top.

3 Try to blow up the balloon. What else is in the bottle? Draw a conclusion.

Science Skill

To draw a conclusion about what happened, think about what you observed.

Gases

Gases are matter. A **gas** does not have a shape of its own. It spreads out to fill its container and take its shape.

Observing Gases

Gases are all around you. Air is made up of different gases. You can not see most gases, but you can see what they do.

A gas fills up the space inside a balloon. A fan makes air blow your hair.

Some gases, like the gas in this soft drink, can mix with water. You can see bubbles in the soft drink as the gas comes out.

Like all matter, gases take up space. Air takes up space in this cup, so no water can come in.

Think About It

1. What are gases?
2. What can we observe about gases?

LESSON 5

How Can We Change Objects?

Investigate

Changing Paper

You will need

4 cards with slits   paints and brushes   glitter   glue   paper and pencil

1 Observe the cards. Record how they look and feel.

2 How could you change the way the cards look and feel? Investigate your ideas.

3 Record how you change the cards.

Science Skill

To investigate, think of changes you could make, and then try them out.

E20

Changing Objects

You can **change** objects, or make them different. You can change their shape, size, color, or texture.

Observing Changes

You can change objects in different ways. You can roll or bend some objects to change their shape.

■ **How can you change clay from a lump into coils that stack?**

You can change some liquids by freezing them. Freezing changes fruit juice into a frozen ice pop.

You can change an object by mixing it with other things. You might make a rock animal for fun. It might be a mix of the rock, paint, and other things.

■ **How did someone change this rock to look like a spider?**

Think About It

1. What are some things you can change about objects?
2. What are three things you can do to objects to change them?

What Happens When Objects Are Taken Apart?

Wheels and an Axle

You will need

2 paper plates

ballpoint pen

1 Make a model of two wheels and an axle. Poke the pen through the plates. Do the plate wheels roll?

CAUTION Be careful. The pen point is sharp!

2 Take apart the wheels and axle. Do the wheels roll? Draw a conclusion.

Science Skill
When you make a model of something, you can use it to find out how the real thing works.

Objects and Their Parts

Many objects are made of parts.
The parts work together to make the
objects work. Without all their parts,
many objects will not work.

How Parts Work Together

A camera must have film to work. Without film, you can not take photographs. A plane must have fuel to fly. Without fuel, the plane's engine will not run.

Mechanic

Sometimes a car does not work the way it should. A **mechanic** can fix a broken part or put in a new one. Then the car will work the way it should again.

Think About It

1. What happens when objects do not have all their parts?
2. What does a mechanic do if a car part is broken?

Mixing Objects to Make Art

A Spanish artist named Pablo Picasso made this sculpture. He used two everyday objects to show something new. Look at the bicycle seat and handlebars.

- **How does this art look like a bull's head?**

Bull's Head by Pablo Picasso

Think and Do

Choose two or three objects in your classroom. Plan a way to put them together to show something new. Then follow your plan.

E28

How Much Can Ships Carry?

Big ships can carry heavy cargo. On the left you see a ship with no cargo. The red line shows that it is floating high in the water. On the right you see a ship loaded with cargo. You can not see the red line. The ship is floating lower in the water.

Think and Do

Make a foil boat. Put it in the water. Slowly put pennies in your boat. How many pennies can it carry without sinking?

Tell What You Know

1. Use the word *solid*, *liquid*, or *gas* to tell about each picture.

Vocabulary

Use each word to tell about the picture.

2.

matter

3.

float

4.

sink

5.
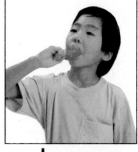
change

6.

mechanic

Using Science Skills

7. Gather and Record Data
Make a chart to gather and record data about liquids. Put one drop of water and one drop of oil on wax paper.

Liquids				
	Makes a Round Drop	Makes a Flat Drop	Can Be Dragged	Can Not Be Dragged
Water				
Oil				

Observe each drop. Use a toothpick to drag each one. Try other liquids and add them to the chart.

8. Draw a Conclusion Think about what makes these cars roll. Draw a conclusion about why one car rolled farther.

Heat and Light

heat

melt

prism

refract

reflect

Did You Know?
The blue part of
a flame gives off
the most heat.

Did You Know?
Your hand gives off enough heat to **melt** some solids.

What Is Heat?

What Heat Does to Water

You will need

| 2 cups with water | 2 thermometers | paper and pencil | clock |

1 Measure the temperature of the water in each cup.

2 Make a chart. Write a number to show each temperature.

3 Wait 10 minutes. Read and record each temperature.

4 Draw a conclusion.

Science Skill

Use numbers to tell what you found out. Compare the numbers. Draw a conclusion.

Heat

Heat can make things warmer. The sun gives off heat. The sun's heat warms the Earth's land, air, and water.

Other Things That Give Off Heat

Fire also gives off heat. Heat from a fire warms the people sitting around it.

■ **How is the fire being used in this picture?**

Rubbing Makes Heat

Almost anything gives off heat if you rub it. Try rubbing your hands together. Can you feel the heat they give off?

■ **What is this boy doing to make heat?**

Think About It

1. What does heat do?
2. What are some things that give off heat?

How Does Heat Change Matter?

How Heat Changes Water

You will need

food coloring

hot water in a bowl

cold water in a bowl

paper and pencil

1 Gather data about how heat changes water. Put a drop of food coloring in cold water. Record.

2 Put a drop of food coloring in hot water. Record.

 Be careful. Hot!
CAUTION

3 How did heat change the water? Tell what you found out.

Science Skill

To gather data about something, observe it. Then draw or write to record your observations.

How Heat Changes Matter

Heat changes matter. It makes a solid melt and a liquid evaporate. It makes a gas spread out.

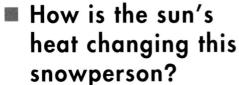 **How is the sun's heat changing this snowperson?**

What Heat Does to Matter

You can observe what heat does to matter. You can heat solids such as ice or sugar to melt them. When solids **melt**, they turn into liquids.

You can heat a liquid, such as soup. Some of it will evaporate, or change to a gas.

■ **What does heat do to these solids and liquids?**

You can heat a gas, such as air.
Hot air spreads out to fill this balloon.

Think About It

1. How does heat change a solid like ice?
2. How does heat change liquids and gases?

What Is Light?

Light and Color

You will need

prism

objects

paper and pencil

crayons or markers

flashlight

 1 Shine a light. Look at objects through the prism.

2 Draw a picture of what you observe. Label it with the colors you observe.

3 Use your picture to communicate what you observed.

Science Skill

To communicate, use the labeled picture to talk about what you observed.

Light

Light lets us see. The sun gives off light as well as heat. The sun's light helps us see what is around us.

Other Things That Give Off Light

Many things besides the sun give off both light and heat. We can use their light to see when there is no sunlight.

■ **What are some things that give off both light and heat?**

Light and Color

Light is made of colors. You can see the colors when light passes through a prism. A **prism** is any clear object that breaks light into colors.

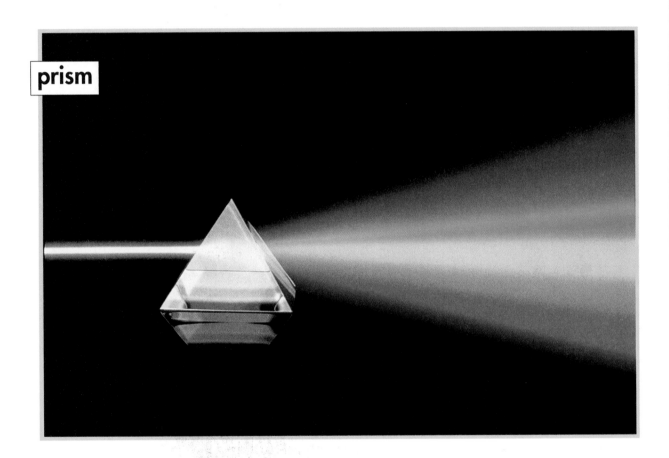

prism

Think About It

1. What does light do?
2. When can you see the colors light is made of?

What Can Light Do?

 Investigate

Making Light Bounce

You will need

flashlight
with battery

index card
in clay

mirror

1 Turn the flashlight on. Observe the light.

2 Put the mirror in front of the light. Move the mirror. Observe.

3 Investigate this problem. How can you make light shine on the card without moving the card?

Science Skill

To investigate a problem, you plan and try different ideas.

How Light Moves

Light moves in a straight line until it hits a solid or a liquid. Dust in the air helps us see light's straight lines.

What Light Can Do

When light hits something solid, it **reflects**, or bounces off in a new direction.

Light reflecting off a cat lets us see the cat. The cat's shadow shows where the cat blocks the light.

■ **What makes the cat's shadow?**

Light passes through water as well as air. Light may bend, or **refract**, where water and air meet. An object that is partly in water may look bent.

■ **What happens to light when it hits a mirror?**

Think About It

1. In what way does light move?
2. What can light do?

A Hot Air Balloonist Explores

Jetta Schantz flies hot air balloons. To go up, she heats the air in her balloon. The hot air in it spreads out and gets lighter. The cool air pushes it up and lifts the balloon.

Think and Do

Observe how hot air spreads out. Blow up a balloon about halfway, and tie it. Use a string to measure around it. Hold the balloon in hot water for a few minutes. Measure again.

 **Math Link**

Measure Shadows

Children in many places have fun with shadows. Children in Indonesia make deer shadow puppets. They sing songs about what their puppets do.

Think and Do

With a partner, make shadow puppets on paper. How can you make them smaller or larger? Trace two shadows. Measure them with paper clips. Find the difference between the two.

Tell What You Know

1. Use the word *light* or *heat* to tell about each picture.

Vocabulary

Tell which picture goes with each word.

a.

b.

2. prism

3. refract

4. melt

5. reflect

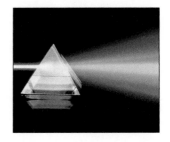

c.

d.

Using Science Skills

6. **Gather Data** Does a foam cup or a metal cup keep cocoa hotter over time? Gather your own data, or read the data in the chart. Use the data to decide which cup to use.

Which Cup Keeps Cocoa Hotter?			
Kind of Cup	Temperature at Start	After 5 Minutes	After 10 Minutes
Foam Cup	55 degrees Celsius	49 degrees Celsius	47 degrees Celsius
Metal Cup	55 degrees Celsius	47 degrees Celsius	43 degrees Celsius

7. **Use Numbers** Tape two mirrors together. Put a small object between them. Count how many times you see the object. Then move the mirrors. Make them show the object only once.

Make Juice Bars

Change liquid juice into a solid by making juice pops.

1. Have a family member help you pour fruit juice into an ice cube tray.

2. Put a toothpick into each part of the tray. *Be careful. Toothpicks are sharp.*

3. Freeze and eat!

Floating Drops

1. Fill jar with salad oil.

2. Put two or three drops of food coloring into the oil. Put the lid on the jar.

3. Tip the jar. What happens to the colored drops? Talk about what floats and why.

Be a Shadow Tracker

1. In the morning, put a sheet of paper by a sunny window.
2. Put a stick in a ball of clay on the paper. Trace the stick's shadow. Write the time.
3. Trace the shadow and write the time again two more times that day.
4. Tell what happens to the shadow.

What Keeps Cold In?

1. Put one ice cube in a foam cup. Put another foam cup on top of that cup.
2. Do the same thing using two clear plastic cups.
3. Put both sets of cups in a warm place.
4. Observe the ice cubes in one hour. Which cups would you use to keep a drink cold?

WRITING

Tab Book On separate sheets of paper, write about solids, liquids, and gases. Add a label to each page. Put your pages together to make a book.

READING

Day Light, Night Light by Franklyn M. Branley Read about different places light comes from. Find the page that shows heat about to change a solid.

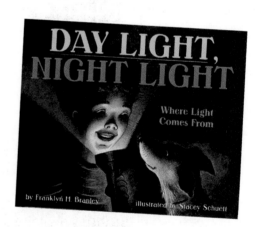

COMPUTER CENTER
Visit *The Learning Site* at www.harcourtschool.com

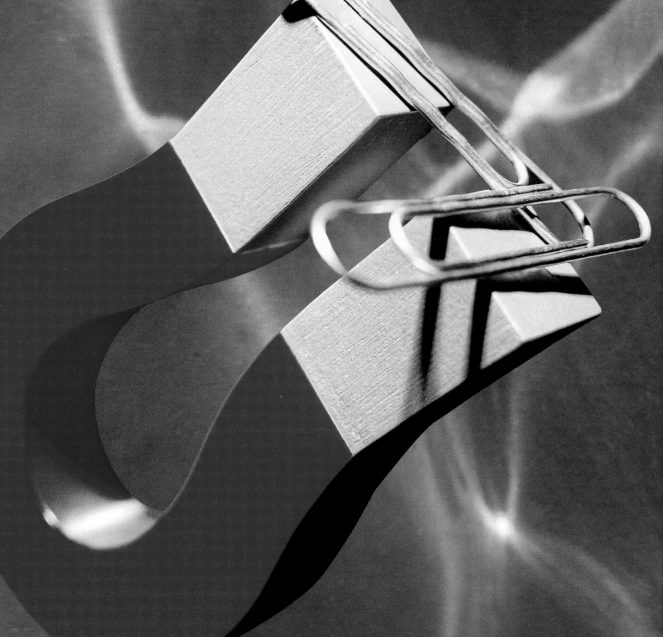

Energy and Forces

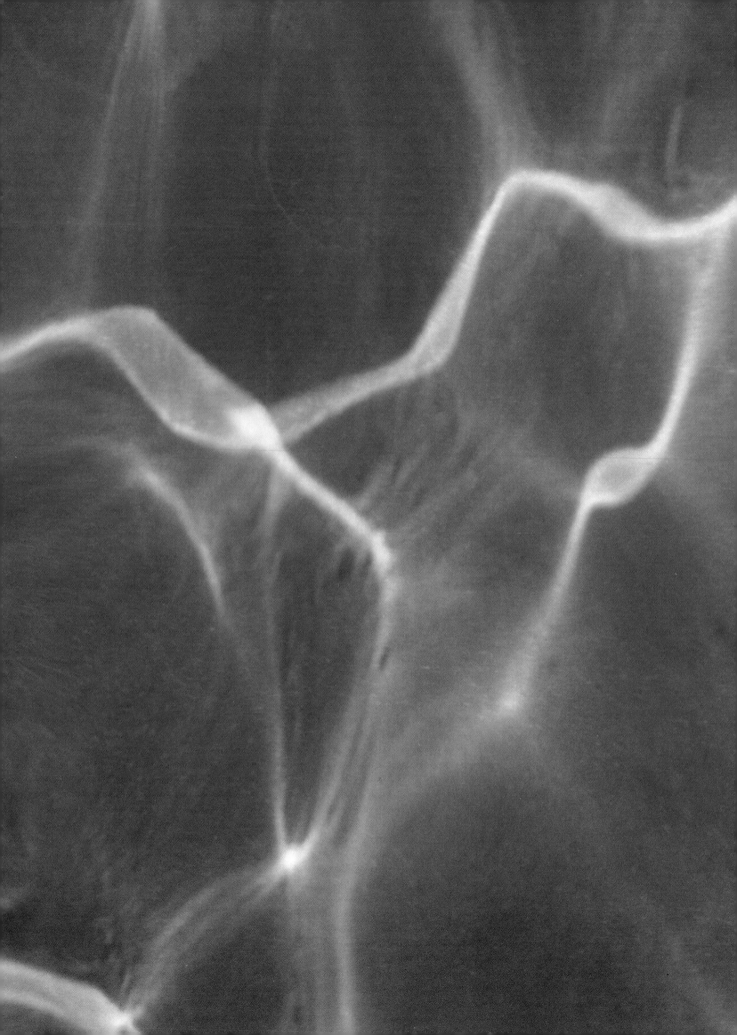

Physical Science

Energy and Forces

UNIT PROJECT

Around the Town

Make a town. Use magnets to make things move.

Pushes and Pulls

Vocabulary

force
push
pull
zigzag
motion
surface
friction
wheel

Did You Know?
Tree roots can **push** a rock when they grow.

Did You Know?

The golden wheel spider can roll like a **wheel**.

What Makes Things Move?

Pushes and Pulls

You will need

small block

things to make the block move

paper and pencil

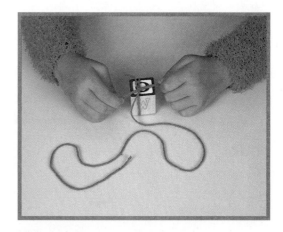

1 What could you do to push or pull the block?

2 Write a plan to investigate your ideas. Then follow your plan.

3 Tell what you used to move the block. Use the word *push* or *pull.*

Science Skill

You investigate by thinking of ideas and trying them out.

Making Things Move

A **force** is a push or a pull. When you **push** something, you press it away. When you **pull** something, you tug it closer.

push

pull

Pushes and Pulls

Pushes and pulls make things move or stop moving. A tow truck pulls a car to the repair shop. A player pushes with a glove to stop a moving ball.

■ **Would the player use a push or a pull to throw the ball?**

A push or a pull can make something change direction. When you kick a ball, you are using a push. First the ball rolls to you. Your push makes it change direction. Then it moves away from you.

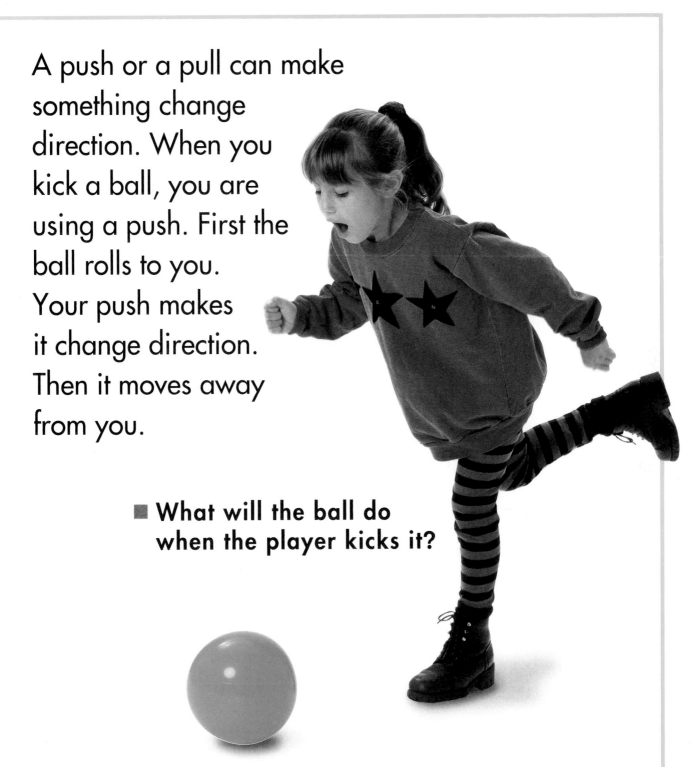

■ **What will the ball do when the player kicks it?**

Think About It

1. What is a force?

2. What can pushes and pulls do?

What Are Some Ways Things Move?

Investigate

Moving Objects

You will need

objects

paper and pencil

1 Observe and record how each object moves when you push or pull it.

2 Group objects that move the same way. Write how you grouped them.

Science Skill

To group the objects, put those that move in the same way together.

Ways Things Move

Pushes and pulls make things move in different ways. Tell what you know about how these rides move.

Telling How Things Move

There are different ways to tell how things move. One way is by the path they make. A car moves in a straight path. A skier may **zigzag**, or make sharp turns back and forth.

Another way to tell how things move is by their speed. Two bikers may start at the same time. If one moves ahead, he or she is moving faster.

Some things move the same way over and over. A top spins round and round. A swing moves back and forth.

■ **What kind of force keeps a swing moving?**

Think About It

1. What are some ways things move?
2. How can you tell if one thing is moving faster than another?

LESSON 3

Why Do Things Move the Way They Do?

Investigate

Predicting Motion

You will need

ramp

plastic ball

tape

block

1 Set up the ramp. Predict where the ball will stop. Mark that place with tape.

2 Let the ball roll down the ramp. Was your prediction right?

3 Now put the block where the ball will hit it. Do Step 2 again.

Science Skill

To predict where the ball will stop, think about how a ball rolls and bounces.

Why Things Move the Way They Do

Moving from one place to another is **motion**. You can observe the motion of an object. This will help you predict where it will move next.

Changing Motion

A push or pull can change the motion of something. A hockey puck moves straight ahead unless something changes its motion.

Different kinds of pushes change how far the puck moves. A hard push moves the puck far. A gentle push moves it only a short way.

■ What kind of push should the player use to move the puck a short way?

Changing Direction

A force can change the direction in which an object moves. A ball will roll in one direction until something pushes it and makes it change.

■ **What does the paddle do to the ball in table tennis?**

Bumps are the pushes that change the direction of bumper boats. When you bump your boat against another boat, your boat bounces back.

Think About It

1. What is motion?
2. What can change the motion of something?

How Do Objects Move on Surfaces?

Smooth and Rough Surfaces

You will need

ramp

toy truck

meterstick

paper and pencil

1 Set up a ramp on a smooth surface. Let the truck roll down.

2 Measure how far it rolls. Record the number. Do the same on a rough surface.

3 On which surface does the truck roll farther? Use your numbers to tell.

Science Skill

Measure how far the truck rolls from the end of the ramp to where the truck stops.

Different Surfaces

A **surface** is the top or outside of something. This floor has both a smooth surface and a rough surface. The truck moves in a different way on each surface.

More Friction, Less Friction

When two surfaces rub together, they make friction. **Friction** is a force that makes it harder to move things.

A rough surface makes more friction than a smooth one. On a rough road, a bike is harder to move. You have to push harder on the pedals.

■ **What surfaces rub together when you ride a bike over a road?**

You can change how much friction a surface makes. If you cover a surface with something wet, it makes less friction. If you cover a surface with something rough, it makes more friction.

Think About It

1. What is friction?
2. What kind of surface makes more friction? What kind makes less friction?

How Do Wheels Help Objects Move?

Investigate

Rollers

You will need

rollers

heavy book

toy truck

tape

1 Push the book. Then put rollers under it. Push again. Which is easier?

2 Push the truck. Tape the wheels, and push it again. Which is easier?

3 Draw a conclusion about wheels and rollers.

Science Skill

To draw a conclusion about something, use what you have observed to explain what happens.

What Wheels Can Do

A roller is any object that rolls. A **wheel** is a roller that turns on an axle. Rollers and wheels make things easier to push or pull.

Many Ways to Use Wheels

People use wheels in many ways. They use baskets on wheels to carry things when they shop. They use chairs on wheels to help them move around. Some children put wheels on boxes to make play cars.

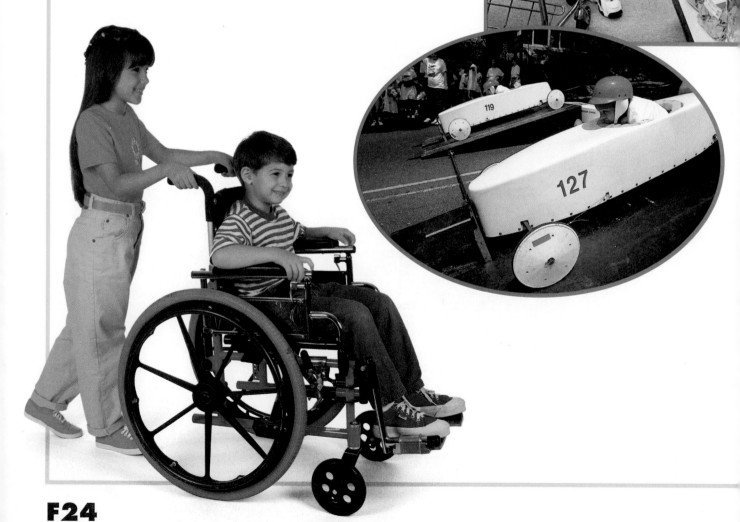

People use wheels to help them push or pull loads. A dolly's wheels make it easy to push heavy boxes. Many suitcases have wheels so that people can pull them along.

■ **Why do people use things that have wheels?**

Think About It

1. What is a wheel?
2. What can wheels do?

Social Studies/Career Link

An Architect Plans Buildings

I. M. Pei designs buildings. He knows about forces that push and pull. He designs buildings that won't fall down.

Think and Do

Use index cards to build a house. Then blow on your house of cards. Find different ways to make a house you can not blow down.

Math Link

Push for Points

In some games, players use pushes to score points. Air hockey and bowling are two games like this.

Think and Do

Make a game that uses pushes to score points. Use a box lid. Then use a pencil to flip a bottle cap ten times into the lid.

Add the number it lands on to your score each time.

Tell What You Know

1. Tell what you know about the picture. Use the words *force, motion, surface,* and *friction.*

Vocabulary

Tell which picture goes with each word.

2. push

3. pull

4. zigzag

5. wheel

a.

b.

c.

d.

Using Science Skills

6. Measure Pull a rock across rough and smooth surfaces with a rubber band. Measure how long the rubber band stretches each time. Make a chart. Record the numbers. Which makes more friction?

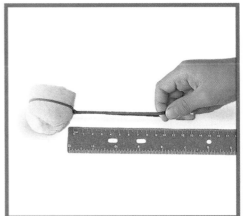

Friction on Surfaces	
Surface	How Long the Rubber Band Stretches
rough	
smooth	

7. Draw a Conclusion Rub your hands together. Feel the friction. Then put a few drops of oil on your hands. Rub again. Draw a conclusion.

Magnets

magnet

attract

strength

repel

poles

magnetic force

magnetize

Did You Know?
The Maglev train is run by **magnets**.

Did You Know?
These magnets can **repel** each other.

What Are Magnets?

 Investigate

What a Magnet Can Do

You will need

bar magnet   objects   paper and pencil

What a Magnet Can Do		
Object	Pulls	Does Not Pull

1 Gather data about the magnet. Hold it near each object.

2 Make a chart like this one. Record what you observe.

3 Group the objects the magnet pulls and those it does not pull.

Science Skill

To gather data about what a magnet can do, observe and record what it does.

Magnets

A **magnet** is a piece of iron that can **attract**, or pull, things. The things it pulls must also be made of iron. Iron is a kind of metal.

■ **How are magnets used here?**

How People Use Magnets

People use magnets to hold things closed and to lift things. They also use them in televisions and electric motors.

A farmer may put a magnet in a cow's stomach. The magnet attracts bits of metal that the cow may eat. This keeps the metal from hurting the cow.

cow magnet

Where Magnets Can Be Found

Some magnets are found in nature. Lodestone is a kind of magnet found in the ground.

lodestone

■ How are the children using magnets in this fishing game?

How Magnets Are the Same and Different

Magnets are the same in one way. They attract objects made of iron. They do not attract objects made of other materials.

Magnets may be different in other ways. They may be round or square, big or small, straight or curved. They may be different colors.

Magnets may be different in **strength**, or how strongly they pull. One magnet may attract more paper clips than another.

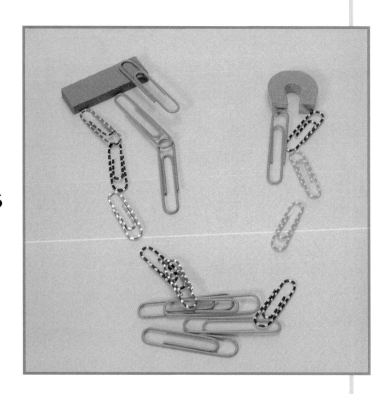

■ **Look at the chart. Which magnet has the greater strength?**

Magnet Strength	
Magnet	Number of Clips
bar magnet	6
horseshoe magnet	3

Think About It

1. What is a magnet?
2. What are some ways people use magnets?

LESSON 2

What Are the Poles of a Magnet?

Investigate

A Magnet's Ends

You will need

bar magnet

paper clips

paper and pencil

1 Pick up paper clips with one end of the magnet. Record the number. Then do the other end.

2 Pick up paper clips with the middle of the magnet. Record the number.

3 Make a bar graph. Infer which parts of the magnet are strongest.

Science Skill

To infer which parts of the magnet are the strongest, compare the numbers in your bar graph.

The Poles of a Magnet

A magnet has two **poles**. These are the places where its pulling force is strongest. Where are the poles of this bar magnet? How can you tell?

What Poles Can Do

Every magnet has a north pole and a south pole. They are often called the *N* pole and the *S* pole.

Two poles that are different attract each other. An *N* pole and an *S* pole attract each other.

Two poles that are the same **repel**, or push away, each other. Two *N* poles repel each other.

■ **What do you think two *S* poles would do?**

Bits of iron can show where a magnet's pull is strongest. The iron bits make a pattern around the magnet. More bits go to the poles, where the pull is strongest.

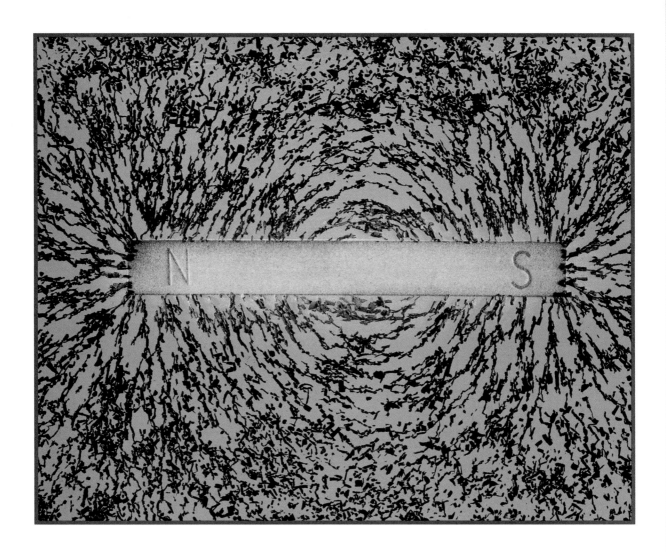

Think About It

1. What are poles?
2. What do poles do?

What Can a Magnet Pull Through?

 Investigate

Things Magnets Pull Through

You will need

bar magnet　　　　　paper clips　　　　　different materials

1 Can a magnet attract paper clips through things? Plan an investigation to find out. Write your plan.

2 Follow your plan to investigate your ideas. Record what you observe.

3 Use your data to communicate what you find out.

Science Skill

To investigate what things a magnet can pull through, first make a plan and then try your ideas.

The Force of a Magnet

A magnet's pull is called **magnetic force**. This force can pass through some things to attract iron objects.

■ **What material is magnetic force passing through to attract these puppets?**

Observing Magnetic Force

The magnetic force of a magnet can pass through paper. It can also pass through water and glass.

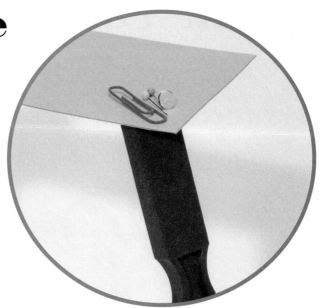

■ **What do you think might happen if the glass were thicker?**

Magnetic force is strong close to a magnet. It can pull a paper clip through the air. Farther away, it may not be strong enough to do this.

Think About It

1. What is magnetic force?
2. What are some materials magnetic force can pass through?

How Can You Make a Magnet?

Making a Magnet

You will need

magnet

2 paper clips

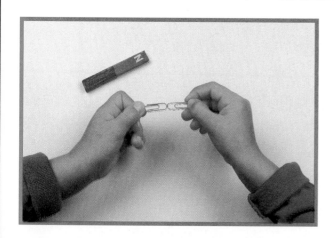

1 Touch one clip to the other. Observe.

3 Take away the magnet. Draw a conclusion. How can you make a magnet?

2 Use the magnet to pick up one clip. Touch that clip to the other one. Observe.

Science Skill

To draw a conclusion, use what you have observed to form an idea.

Making a Magnet

A magnet can **magnetize**, or give magnetic force to, things it attracts. The magnet on this crane has magnetized some pieces of metal. Their new magnetic force attracts more pieces.

Ways to Make a Magnet

You can magnetize an iron nail. Stroke the nail on the magnet ten times the same way. Then the nail will be magnetized for a short time.

■ How can you tell that this nail is now a magnet?

Some magnets are made from iron heated with other materials. These magnets are made in a factory.

A magnet engineer finds new ways to make magnets. These magnets may be stronger or last longer than iron ones.

Think About It

1. What can you use to magnetize an object made of iron?
2. How can you make a magnet?

Math Link

Measure Magnetic Force

You can compare the strengths of different magnets. To do this, you will need to record how far their magnetic forces reach.

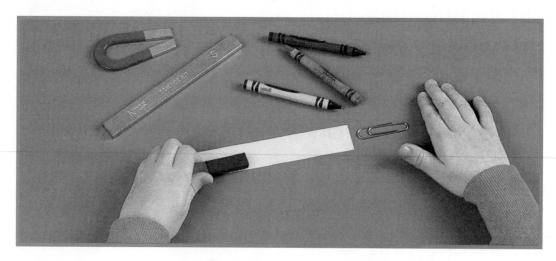

Think and Do

Lay a paper clip at one end of a paper strip. Hold one magnet at the other end. Slide the magnet slowly toward the clip. Make a mark to show where the magnet is when the clip moves.

Do the same thing with each magnet. Which magnet is the strongest?

Compass Readings

Long ago, travelers used compasses to find their way. Travelers still use them today. A compass has a magnetized needle that always points north.

Think and Do

Make your own compass. Float a plastic plate in water. Place a bar magnet in the center of the plate. Turn the plate. Which way is north?

Tell What You Know

1. Use the words *strength*, *poles*, and *magnetic force* to tell about each picture.

 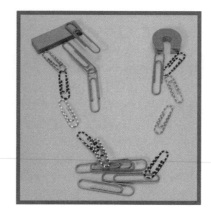 

Vocabulary

Tell which picture goes with each word.

2. magnet

3. attract

4. repel

5. magnetize

a.

b.

c.

d.

Using Science Skills

6. Infer Look at the two patterns made by the bits of iron. Which magnet made each pattern? How do you know?

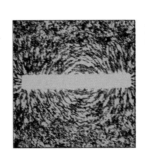

7. Investigate Some people use a metal detector to help them find things made of metal.

Play a metal detector game. Ask a partner to put three metal objects in a group of objects.

Predict which objects your magnet will attract. Investigate to find out.

Magnetic Kite

1. Cut out a tissue paper kite.

2. Attach thread and a paper clip.

3. Tape the thread's tail to a table.

4. Use the magnet to pick up your kite without touching it.

Magnetic Race-Car Game

1. Draw a road on cardboard.

2. Put two paper clips on the road.

3. Put two magnets under the cardboard. Move the magnets to race your clips.

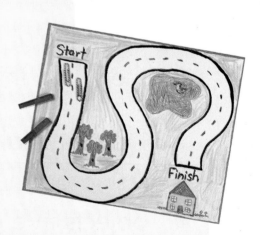

Make a Water Wheel

1. Push toothpicks into the ends of a piece of clay. *Be careful. Toothpicks are sharp.*

2. Push strips cut from a carton into the clay to make a water wheel.

3. Hold the wheel by the toothpicks. Place the wheel under running water.

4. Tell how the water makes the wheel turn.

Marble Fun Slide

1. Tape together paper towel tubes to make a fun slide.

2. Use books to hold up the tubes.

3. Put a marble at the top, and listen to it race to the bottom. Talk about how it moves.

WRITING

Accordion Book
Make a book that you pull to open and push to close! On each page, write about a push or pull.

READING

What Makes a Magnet?
by Franklyn M. Branley
Read more about magnets. Tell two ways people use them.

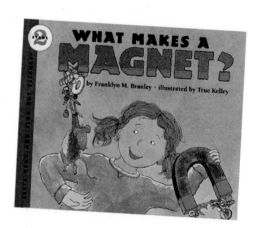

COMPUTER CENTER
Visit *The Learning Site* at
www.harcourtschool.com

References

Investigating

This plan will help you work like a scientist.

STEP 1 — Ask a question.

Which car will roll the farthest?

STEP 2 — Make a prediction.

I predict this car will win.

STEP 3 — Plan a fair test.

I'll start each car at the same spot.

STEP 4—Do your test.

I'll measure how far each car rolls.

STEP 5—Draw a conclusion.

My prediction was correct! This car rolled the farthest.

Investigate More

I wonder if the height of the ramp will make a difference.

Using Science Tools

Hand Lens

1. Hold the hand lens close to your face
2. Move the object until you see it clearly.

Thermometer

1. Place the thermometer.
2. Wait two minutes.
3. Find the top of the liquid in the tube.
4. Read the number.

The temperature is 40 degrees.

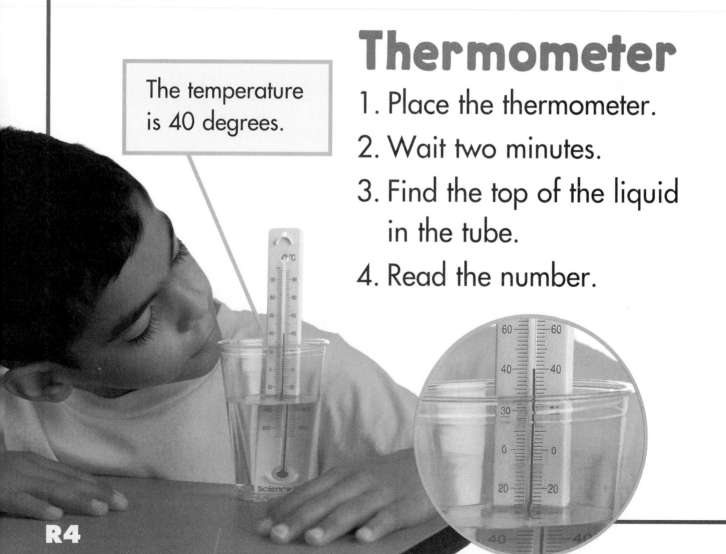

Ruler

1. Put the edge of the ruler at the end of the object.

2. Look at the number at the other end.

3. Read how long the object is.

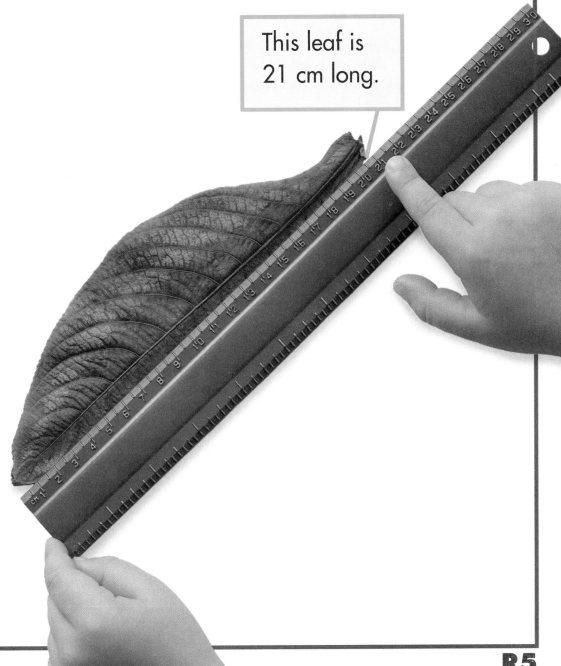

This leaf is 21 cm long.

Measuring Cup

1. Pour the liquid into the cup.
2. Put the cup on a table.
3. Wait until the liquid is still.
4. Look at the level of the liquid.
5. Read how much liquid there is.

There are 150 milliliters of liquid here.

Clock

It is 10:00.

1. Look at the hour hand.
2. Look at the minute hand.
3. Read the time.

Stopwatch

Now 15 seconds have gone by.

1. To start timing, press START.
2. To stop timing, press STOP.
3. Read how much time has passed.

Balance

1. Start with the pans even.
2. Put the object in one pan.
3. Add masses until the pans are even again.
4. Count up the number of masses.

Computer

1. A computer can help you draw.

2. Most computers help you find answers to questions.

3. Many computers help you communicate.

Measurements

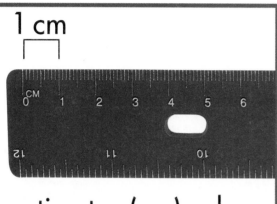

1 cm

centimeter (cm) ruler

1 in.

inch (in.) ruler

Water freezes at 32°F. —— Water freezes at 0°C.

Fahrenheit (F)
temperature

Celsius (C)
temperature

1 kilogram (kg)

1 pound (lb)

1 liter (L)

1 cup (c)

Health Handbook

Caring for Your Body

Staying Safe

Eyes and Ears

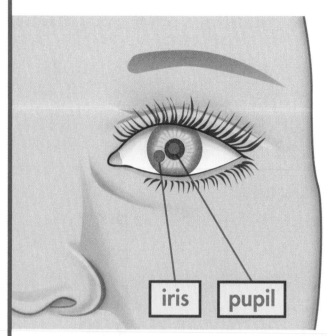

Outside of Eye

iris   pupil

Caring for Your Eyes and Ears

• Some bright light can hurt your eyes. Never look at the sun or at very bright lights.

• Never put an object in your ear.

Eyes

When you look at your eyes, you can see a white part, a colored part, and a dark center. The colored part is the iris. The dark center is the pupil.

Inside of Eye

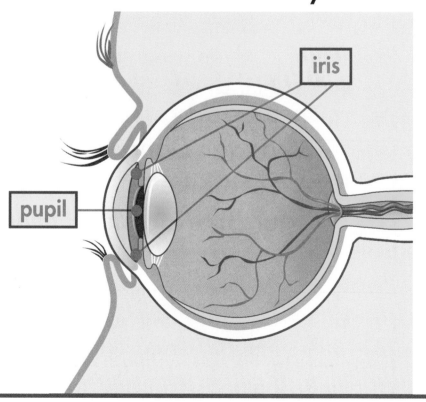

iris

pupil

Ear

Your ears let you hear. Most of each ear is inside your head.

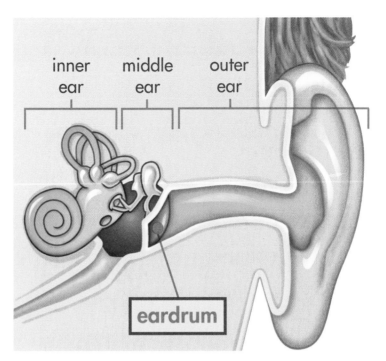

inner ear   middle ear   outer ear

eardrum

Inside of Ear   **Outside of Ear**

ACTIVITIES

1. The iris of the eye may be different colors. Look at the eyes of your classmates. How many colors do you see?

2. Ask a classmate to stand across the classroom from you. Have him or her say your name in a normal voice. Now put a hand behind each ear and have him or her say your name again in the same voice. Which time sounded louder?

The Skeletal System

Inside your body are hard, strong bones. They make up your skeleton. Your skeleton holds you up.

Caring for Your Skeletal System

Protect your head. Wear a helmet when you ride your bike.

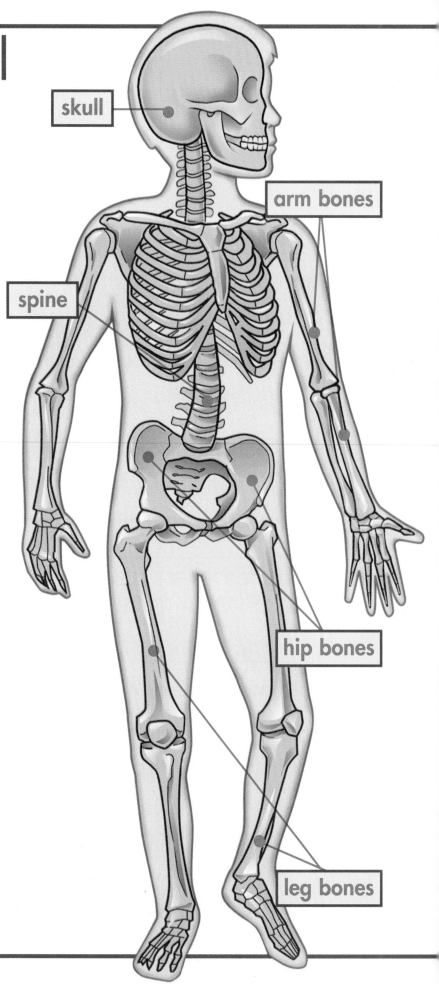

skull

arm bones

spine

hip bones

leg bones

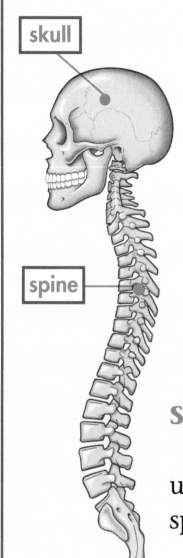

skull

spine

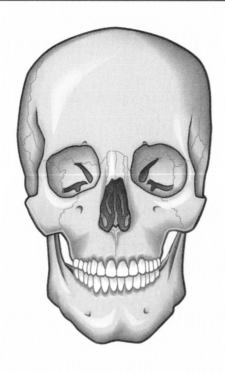

Skull

The bones in your head are called your skull. Your skull protects your brain.

Spine

Your spine, or backbone, is made up of many small bones. Your spine helps you stand up straight.

ACTIVITIES

1. Look at a bike helmet. How is it like your skull?

2. Your foot is about the same length as your arm between your hand and your elbow. Put your foot on your arm and check it out!

The Digestive System

Your digestive system helps your body get energy from the food you eat.

Caring for Your Digestive System

- Brush and floss your teeth every day.
- Don't eat right before you exercise. Your body needs energy to digest food.

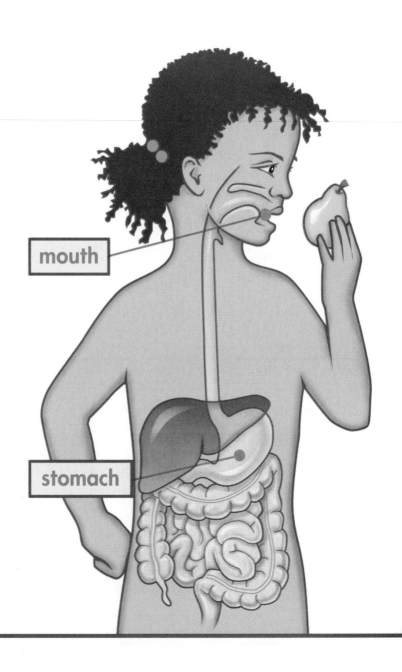

mouth

stomach

Teeth

Some of your teeth tear food and some grind it into small parts.

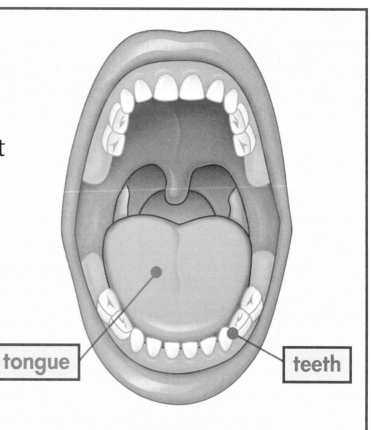

tongue

teeth

Tongue

Your tongue helps you swallow food. It is a strong muscle that also lets you taste.

ACTIVITIES

1. Bite into an apple and chew the bite. Which teeth did you use for these jobs?

2. Lick a salty pretzel and a lollipop. Which one can you taste better with just the tip of your tongue?

The Circulatory System

Blood goes through your body in your circulatory system. Your heart pumps the blood. Your blood vessels carry the blood.

Caring for Your Circulatory System

- Exercise every day to keep your heart strong.
- Keep germs out of your blood. Wash cuts with soap and water. Never touch someone else's blood.

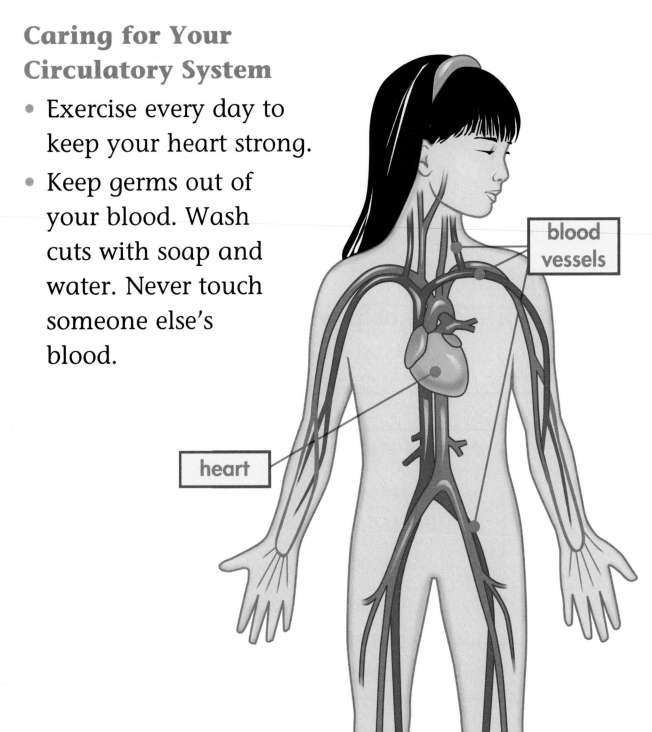

blood vessels

heart

Heart

Your heartbeat is the sound of your heart pumping. Your heart is about the same size as a fist.

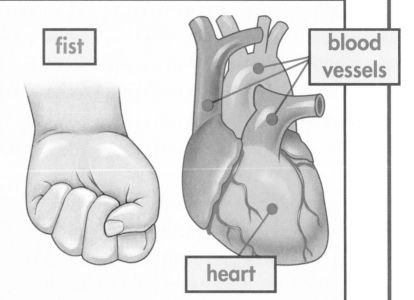

fist

blood vessels

heart

Blood Vessels

Blood vessels are tubes that carry blood through your body.

ACTIVITIES

1. Ask an adult to blow up a hot-dog shaped balloon so that it is not quite full. Squeeze one end. What happens?

2. Put your ear to the middle of a classmate's chest and listen to the heartbeat. Then listen again through a paper cup with the bottom torn out. Which way of listening works better?

The Respiratory System

When you breathe, you are using your respiratory system. Your mouth, your nose, and your lungs are parts of your respiratory system.

Caring for Your Respiratory System

- Never put anything in your nose.

- Exercise makes you breathe harder and is good for your lungs.

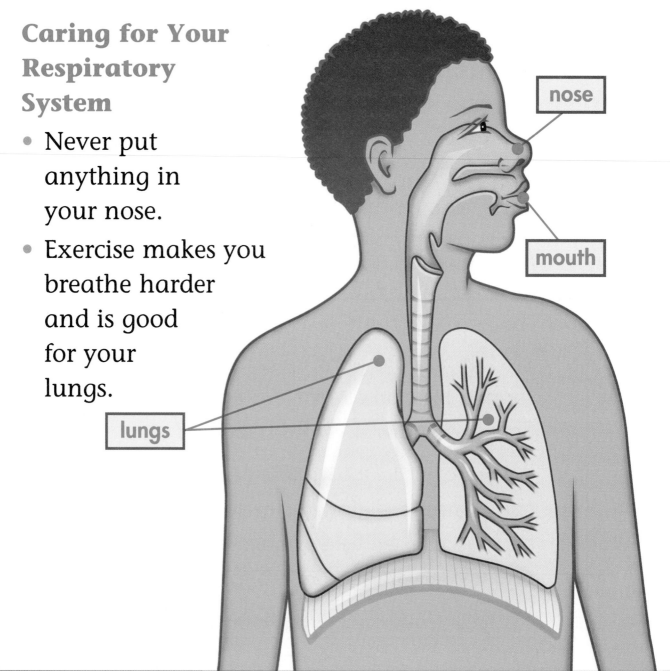

nose

mouth

lungs

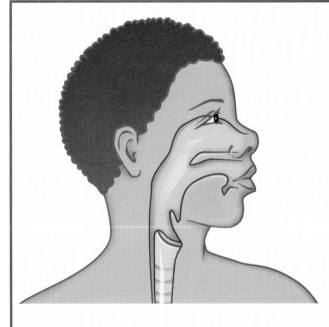

Mouth and Nose

Air goes in and out of your body through your mouth and nose.

Lungs

You have two lungs in your chest. When you breathe in, your lungs fill with air. When you breathe out, air leaves your lungs.

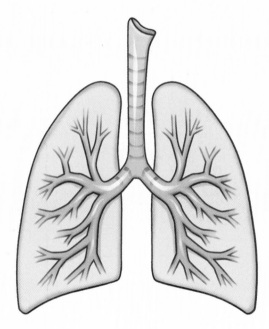

ACTIVITIES

1. Watch your chest and stomach muscles as you take a breath and let it out. Describe what happens.

2. Count how many breaths you take in one minute.

The Muscular System

The muscles in your body help you move.

Caring for Your Muscular System

Warm up your muscles before you play or exercise.

ACTIVITY

Hold your arm straight out from your body and lift it over your head. Then try it again with a book in your hand. How do the muscles in your arm feel?

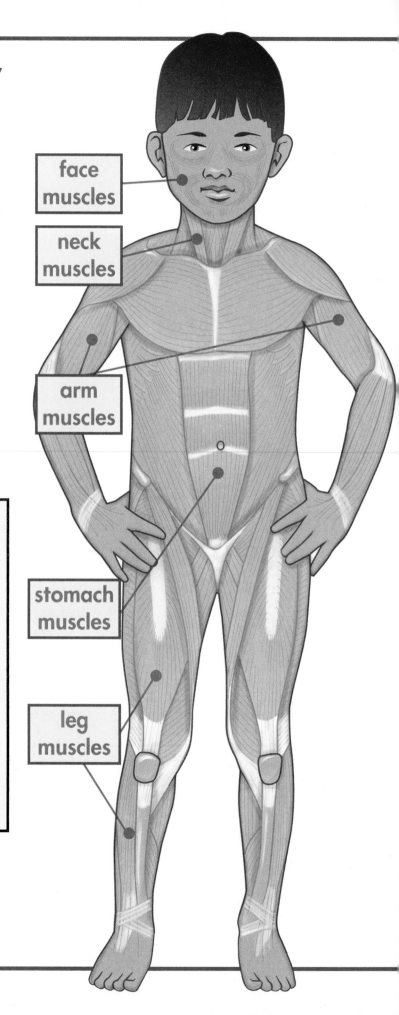

face muscles

neck muscles

arm muscles

stomach muscles

leg muscles

The Nervous System

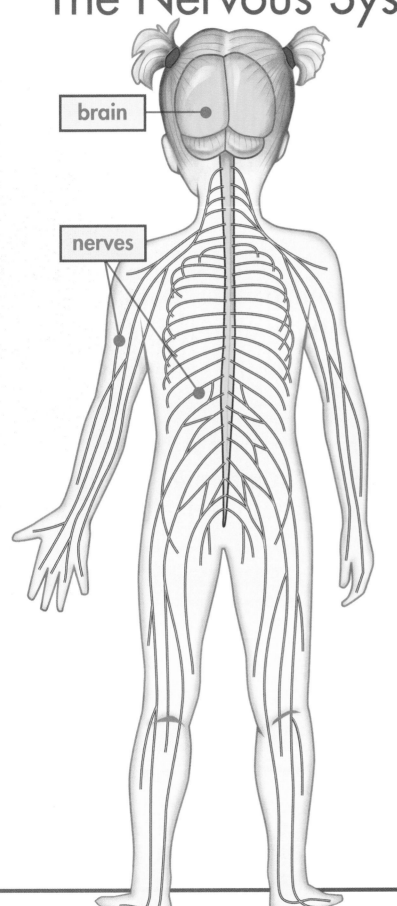

brain

nerves

Your nervous system keeps your body working and tells you about things around you. Your brain is part of your nervous system.

Caring for Your Nervous System

Get plenty of sleep. Sleeping lets your brain rest.

ACTIVITY

Clap your hands in front of a classmate's face. What happens to his or her eyes?

Staying Safe

Fire Safety

You can stay safe from fires. Follow these safety rules.

- Never play with matches or lighters.
- Be careful around stoves, heaters, fireplaces, and grills.
- Don't use microwaves, irons, or toasters without an adult's help.
- Practice your family's fire safety plan.
- If there is a fire in your home, get out quickly. Drop to the floor and crawl if the room is filled with smoke. If a closed door feels hot, don't open it. Use another exit. Call 911 from outside your home.
- If your clothes catch on fire, use Stop, Drop, and Roll right away to put out the flames.

1 Stop Don't run or wave your arms.

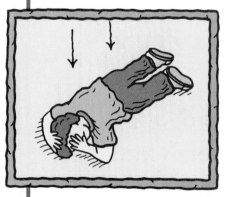

2 Drop Lie down quickly. Cover your eyes with your hands.

3 Roll Roll back and forth to put out the fire.

Stranger Danger

You can stay safe around strangers. Follow these rules.

- Never talk to strangers.
- Never go with a stranger, on foot or in a car.
- If you are home alone, do not open the door. Do not let telephone callers know you are alone.
- Never give your name, address, or phone number to anyone you don't know. (You may give this information to a 911 operator in an emergency.)
- If you are lost or need help, talk to a police officer, a guard, or a store clerk.
- If a stranger bothers you, use the Stranger Danger rules to stay safe.

❶ Say no! Yell if you need to. You do not have to be polite to strangers.

❷ Get away. Walk fast or run in the opposite direction. Go toward people who can help you.

❸ Tell someone. Tell a trusted adult, such as a family member, a teacher, or a police officer. Do not keep secrets about strangers.

Staying Safe
A Safe Bike

To ride your bike safely, you need to start with a safe bike. A safe bike is the right size for you. When you sit on your bike with the pedal in the lowest position, you should be able to rest your heel on the pedal.

After checking the size of your bike, check to see that it has the right safety equipment. Your bike should have everything shown below.

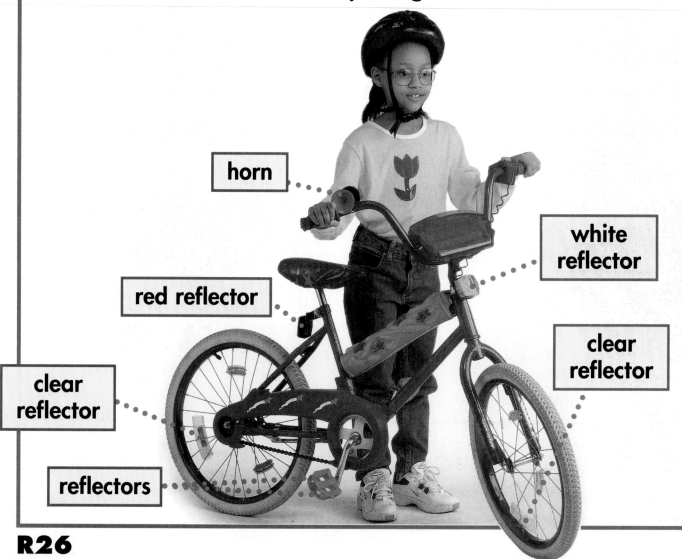

horn

white reflector

red reflector

clear reflector

clear reflector

reflectors

Your Bike Helmet

◀ Always wear a bike helmet. Wear your helmet flat on your head. Be sure it is strapped tightly. If your helmet gets bumped in a fall, replace it right away, even if it doesn't look damaged.

Safety on the Road

- Check your bike for safety every time you ride it.
- Ride in single file. Ride in the same direction as traffic.
- Stop, look, listen, and think when you enter a street or cross a driveway.
- Walk your bike across an intersection.
- Obey all traffic signs and signals.
- Don't ride at night without an adult. Wear light-colored clothing and use lights and reflectors for night riding.

GLOSSARY

Visit the Multimedia Science Glossary to see pictures of these words and to hear the words pronounced: **www.harcourtschool.com/scienceglossary**

A

air
What people breathe but can not see, taste, or smell. (C23)

attract
To pull something. (F33)

algae
An ocean plant. (B40)

C

change
To make different. (E21)

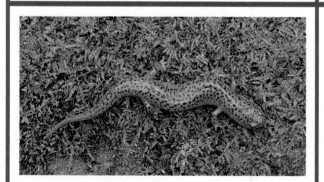

amphibian
An animal with smooth, wet skin. (A52)

condense
To change from water vapor into tiny drops of water. (D18)

R28

desert
A dry place. (B31)

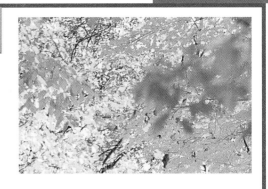

fall
The season that follows summer. (D35)

E

enrich
To make better. (B12)

float
To stay on top of a liquid. (E13)

evaporate
To change from water into water vapor. (D18)

flowers
The part of a plant that makes seeds. (A27)

force

A push or a pull. (F5)

friction

A force that makes it harder to move things. (F20)

forest

A place where many trees grow. (B27)

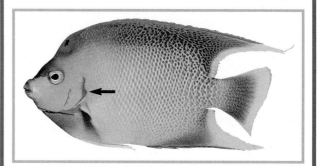

gas

Matter that does not have a shape of its own, such as air. (E17)

fresh water

Water that is not salty. (C27)

gills

Body part that helps a fish take air from water. (A47)

hatch

To break out of an egg. (A60)

heat

What is given off by fire or by the sun. (E35)

insect

An animal that has three body parts and six legs. (A55)

lake

A body of water with land all around it. (C28)

larva

A caterpillar. (A66)

leaves

The plant part that makes food for the plant. (A26)

R31

liquid

Matter that flows to take the shape of its container. (E9)

magnetic force

The pulling force of a magnet. (F43)

living

Need food, water, and air to live and grow. (A11)

magnetize

To give magnetic force to something a magnet attracts. (F47)

magnet

A piece of iron that pulls things made of iron. (F33)

mammal

An animal that has hair or fur and feeds its young milk. (A50)

matter

Everything around you. (E5)

motion

Movement from one place to another. (F13)

mechanic

A person who can fix a broken car part or put in a new one. (E27)

 N

nonliving

Does not need food, water, and air and does not grow. (A11)

melt

To change from a solid to a liquid. (E40)

O

ocean

A large, deep body of salt water. (B39)

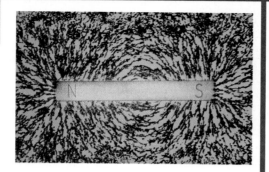

poles

The places where the pulling force of a magnet is strongest. (F39)

product

Something that people make from other things. (B16)

pollen

The powder in flowers that helps flowers make seeds. (B13)

pull

To tug something closer. (F5)

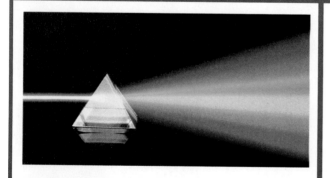

prism

A clear object that breaks light into its colors. (E45)

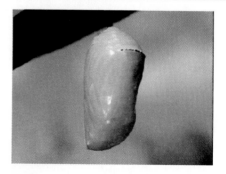

pupa

A hard covering over a caterpillar. (A67)

push

To press something away. (F5)

refract

To bend or change the direction of light. (E49)

rain forest

A forest that is wet all year. (B35)

repel

To push away. (F40)

reflect

To bounce back light. (E48)

reptile

An animal with rough, dry skin. (A52)

river

A body of moving water that is larger than a stream. (C28)

 S

salt water

Water that has salt in it. (C31)

rock

A hard, nonliving thing that comes from the Earth. (C5)

sand

Tiny, broken pieces of rock. (C6)

roots

A plant part that holds plants in the soil and takes in water. (A24)

season

One of four times of the year—fall, winter, spring, and summer. (D27)

seed

What most plants grow from. (A29)

shelter

A place where an animal can be safe. (B8)

seed coat

Covering a seed may have. (A29)

sink

To drop to the bottom of a liquid. (E13)

senses

Touch, sight, smell, hearing, and taste. (A5)

soil

The part of Earth's surface that is made of tiny rocks and bits of dead plants and animals. (C9)

solid

Matter that keeps its shape. (E6)

stream

A body of moving water smaller than a river. (C28)

spring

The season that follows winter. (D27)

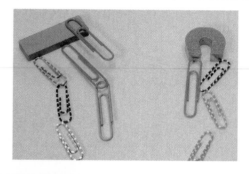

strength

How strong something is, such as a magnet's pull. (F37)

stem

Plant part that helps hold up the plant and moves water to the leaves. (A25)

summer

The season that follows spring. (D31)

sunlight
Light from the sun. (A34)

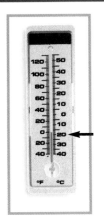

temperature
The measure of how hot or cold something is. (D9)

surface
The top or outside of something. (F19)

texture
How something feels. (C13)

tadpoles
Young frogs that hatch from eggs. (A72)

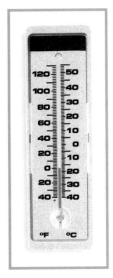

thermometer
A tool that measures temperature. (D9)

water cycle

The movement of water from the Earth to the sky and back again. (D18)

wheel

A roller that turns on an axle. (F23)

water vapor

Water that you can not see in the air. (D18)

wind

Moving air. (D13)

weather

What the air outside is like. (D5)

winter

The season that follows fall. (D39)

Z

zigzag

With sharp turns back and forth. (F10)

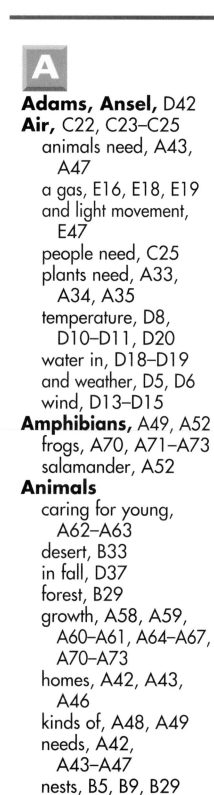

Photography Credits

Page placement key: (t) top, (c) center, (b) bottom, (l) left, (r) right, (bg) background, (i) inset

UNIT A
A02-3: Ron Kimball Photography; A03(inset): Ray Mathis/The Stock Market; A05: Picture It; A06: David Waldorf/FPG International; A08: Laura Dwight Photography; A09(b): Laura Dwight Photography; A09(t): DiMaggio/Kalish/The Stock Market; A11: Gene Peach/Index Stock; A12(l): John Gerlach/Animals Animals / Earth Scenes; A12(r): Mitsuaki Iwago/Minden Pictures; A13(l): Barry L. Runk/Grant Heilman Photography, Inc.; A13(r): Michael Groen Photography; A14(l): Victoria Hurst/Tom Stack & Associates; A14(r): Laura Dwight/Peter Arnold, Inc.; A15(l): Werner H. Muller/Peter Arnold, Inc.; A15(r): Jeff Foott/Bruce Coleman Inc.; A17: Stephen Ogilvy/Picture It ; A18(br): Michael Groen Photography; A18(tc): Sonya Jacobs/The Stock Market; A18(tcl): Michael Groen Photography; A18(tdr): George Mattei/Envision; A18(tl): Tony Freeman/Photo Edit; A18(tr): John Fowler/Valan Photos; A19: Michael Groen Photography; A20: Margaret Gowan/Tony Stone Images; A20-21: Frans Lanting/Minden Pictures; A21(inset): Richard Shiell/Animals Animals/Earth Scenes; A25(r): Bill Bachman/Photo Researchers, Inc.; A26(bl): Colin Milkins/Animals Animals/Earth Scenes; A26(br): Runk/Schoenberger/Grant Heilman Photography, Inc.; A26(tc): Greg Vaughn/Tom Stack & Associates; A26(tl): Runk/Schoenberger/Grant Heilman Photography, Inc.; A26(tr): Don Mason/The Stock Market; A27: Rick Miller/AG Stock USA; A30(bl): Barry L. Runk/Grant Heilman Photography, Inc.; A30(br): Inga Spence/Tom Stack & Associates; A30(cr): Ed Young/Ag Stock; A30(tl): Gerard Lacz/Peter Arnold, Inc.; A30(tr): Ed Young/AG Stock USA; A30-31:Tom Bean/DRK Photo; A31(bl): G. I. Bernard/Animals Animals/Earth Scenes; A31(br): Runk/Schoenberger/Grant Heilman Photography, Inc.; A31(cl): Barry L. Runk/Grant Heilman Photography, Inc.; A31(tl): Runk/Schoenberger/Grant Heilman Photography, Inc.; A31(tr): D. Trask/The Stock Market; A33: Glenn Oakley/AG Stock USA; A35(l): Larry Ulrich/Tony Stone Images; A35(r): Bill Brooks/Masterfile; A36(t): National Gallery, London/Superstock; A38(a): Superstock; A38(b): Jerry Howard/Positive Images; A38(f): D. Cavagnaro/Visuals Unlimited; A38(c): Tim McKenna/The Stock Market; A38(d): Lynwood M. Chase/Photo Researchers, Inc.; A38(e): T.A. Wiewandt/DRK Photo; A38(top-all), 38(g) & 39(b): Runk/Schoenberger/Grant Heilman Photography, Inc.; A39(t): Fred Bruemmer/DRK Photo; A40-41: Kim Taylor/Bruce Coleman Inc.; A41(bl): Michael Fogden/DRK Photo; A41(tl): J. C. Carton/Bruce Coleman Inc.; A41(tr): Hans Reinhard/Bruce Coleman Inc.; A43: S. Nielsen/DRK Photo; A44(bl): Tom Tietz/Tony Stone Images; A44(br): Tom Brakefield/The Stock Market; A44(tl): Dick Canby/DRK Photo; A44(tr): Steve Bly/Tony Stone Images; A45(b): Frans Lanting/Minden Pictures; A45(t): Belinda Wright/DRK Photo; A46(b): Lawrence Migdale/Harcourt/; A46(c): Ralph Ginzburg/Peter Arnold, Inc.; A46(t): Merlin Tuttle/Photo Researchers, Inc.; A47(l): Ken Howard/The Wildlife Collection; A47(r): G. I. Bernard/Animals Animals/Earth Scenes; A49(bcr): Jane Burton/Bruce Coleman Inc.; A49(br): Joe McDonald/Tom Stack & Associates; A49(l): Patricia Doyle/Tony Stone Images; A49(tcr): Lemoine Jacana/Photo Researchers, Inc.; A49(tr): Marian Bacon/Animals Animals/Earth Scenes; A50(bl): Ed Reschke/Peter Arnold, Inc.; A50(br): M. Rutz/Natural Selection; A50(tr): Stephen J. Krasemann/DRK Photo; A51(b): M. H. Sharp/Photo Researchers, Inc.; A51(tl): Anthony Mercieca/Photo Researchers, Inc.; A51(tr): Frans Lanting/Minden Pictures; A52(b): Suzanne L. Collins/Photo Researchers, Inc.; A52(c): Tui de Roy/Minden Pictures; A52(t): David Muench/Tony Stone Images; A53(b): Brian Parker/Tom Stack & Associates; A53(t): Charles V. Angelo/Photo Researchers, Inc.; A55: John Mitchell/Photo Researchers, Inc.; A56(b): Richard L. Carlton/Photo Researchers, Inc.; A56(t): A. Ramage/Animals Animals/Earth Scenes; A57(c): Robert & Linda Mitchell; A57(t): Zefa / Brockhaus/The Stock Market; A59(b): Jane Burton/DK Photos; A59(t): Jane Burton/Bruce Coleman Inc.; A60(br & bl): Jane Burton/DK Photos; A60(tr & tl): Jane Burton/Bruce Coleman Inc.; A61(br, bl): Jane Burton/DK Photos; A61(tl): Jane Burton/Bruce Coleman Inc.; A61(tr): Jane Burton/DK Photos; A62(b): John Giustina/The Wildlife Collection; A62(c): Robert Winslow/Natural Selection; A62(t): Bob Bennett/The Wildlife Collection; A63:Stefan Lundgren/The Wildlife Collection; A65: Mesza/Bruce Coleman Inc.; A66(b): Michael Fogden/DRK Photo; A66(t): Ed Reschke/Peter Arnold, Inc.; A67(b): Harry Rogers/Photo Researchers, Inc.; A67(tl: Jeff Foot/DRK Photo; A67(tr): D. Cavagnaro/DRK Photo; A68(bl): John Fowler/Valan Photos; A68(tl): Sturgis McKeever/Photo Researchers, Inc.; A68-69(c): Gary Vestal/Tony Stone Images; A69(br): Kjell Sandved/Butterfly Alphabet Inc.; A69(tr): Nancy Rotenberg/Animals Animals/Earth Scenes; A71: S. Dalton/Animals Animals/Earth Scenes; A72(c): Runk/Schoenberger/Grant Heilman Photography, Inc.; A72(l): Breck P. Kent/Animals Animals/Earth Scenes; A72(r): John M. Burnley/Photo Researchers, Inc.; A72-73: Michael Groen Photography; A73(l): Runk/Schoenberger/Grant Heilman Photography, Inc.; A73(r): Joe McDonald/Animals Animals/Earth Scenes; A74: Stephen Ogilvy/Picture It; A75(b): Michael Groen Photography; A75(t): Kjell Sandved/Butterfly Alphabet Inc.; A76(1): Patricia Doyle/Tony Stone Images; A76(3): Breck P. Kent/Animals Animals/Earth Scenes; A76(4): David M. Dennis/Tom Stack & Associates; A76(5): Doug Wechsler/Animals Animals/Earth Scenes; A76(6): J. H. Robinson/Animals Animals/Earth Scenes; A77: Gary Vestal/Tony Stone Images;

UNIT B
B02-3: Gregory Ochocki/Photo Researchers, Inc.; B03(l): E.F. Anderson/Visuals Unlimited; B03(r): Roy Morsch/The Stock Market; B05: Lynn M. Stone/Bruce Coleman Inc.; B06(l): Chris Jones/The Stock Market; B06(r): Zefa-Brockhaus/The Stock Market; B07(l): John Chellman/Animals Animals/Earth Scenes; B07(r): Beth Davidow/Visuals Unlimited; B08(r): Raymond A. Mendez/Animals Animals/Earth Scenes; B08(t): Tom Brakefield/DRK Photo; B09(bl): Wendell Metzen/Bruce Coleman Inc.; B09(br): Jeff Foott/Bruce Coleman Inc.; B09(tr): Scott Nielsen/Bruce Coleman Inc.; B12(bl): Breck P. Kent/Animals Animals/Earth Scenes; B12(tr): Patti Murray/Animals Animals/Earth Scenes; B13: Darlyne A. Murawski/Peter Arnold, Inc.; B15: Richard Hutchings/Picture It; B16(b): Pete Saloutos/The Stock Market; B16(c): Aaron Haupt/Photo Researchers, Inc.; B16(t): Jon Feingersh/The Stock Market; B17(bl): Hank Morgan/Rainbow; B17(tr): Stephen Ogilvy/Picture It; B18(bl): Larry Lefever/Grant Heilman Photography, Inc.; B18(br): Michael Groen Photography; B20: Stephen Ogilvy/Picture It; B21(b): Michael Groen Photography; B21(t): Eric Horan; B22(b): Raymond A. Mendez/Animals Animals/Earth Scenes; B22(c): Breck P. Kent/Animals Animals/Earth Scenes; B22(d): Michael Groen Photography; B22(tc): Hans Reinhard/Bruce Coleman Inc.; B22(tl): Tom Bean/DRK Photo; B22(tr): Tom Bean/Bruce Coleman Inc.; B24-25: Jeremy Woodhouse/DRK Photo; B25(inset): Robert P. Carr/Bruce Coleman Inc.; B27: Stephen J. Krasemann/DRK Photo; B28(l): Pat O'Hara/Tony Stone Images; B28(r): James H. Robinson/Animals Animals/Earth Scenes; B29(br): R. A. Simpson/Visuals Unlimited; B29(tl): Art Wolfe/Tony Stone Images; B29(tr): Robert Lubeck/Animals Animals/Earth Scenes; B31: Daniel J. Cox/Natural Exposures; B32(bl): M.P. Kahl/DRK Photo; B32(br): Jeff Foott/DRK Photo; B32(tr): Nora & Rick Bowers/The Wildlife Collection; B33(bl): Joe McDonald/Animals Animals/Earth Scenes; B33(c): Runk/Schoenberger/Grant Heilman Photography, Inc.; B33(tr): Leonard Lee Rue III/Bruce Coleman Inc.; B35: Michael Sewell/Peter Arnold, Inc.; B36(l): Michael Fogden/DRK Photo; B36(r): Ed Wheeler/The Stock Market; B37(b): David Matherly/Visuals Unlimited; B37(t): Softlight Photography/Animals Animals/Earth Scenes; B39: David Hall/Photo Researchers, Inc.; B40(l): Soames Sommerhays/Photo Researchers, Inc.; B40-41: Doug Perrine/DRK Photo; B41(br): Fred Winner/Jacana/Photo Researchers, Inc.; B41(br): Dave B. Fleetham/Visuals Unlimited; B42(tc): Edgar T. Jones/Bruce Coleman Inc.; B42(tl): Sullivan & Rogers/Bruce Coleman Inc.; B42(tr): Patti Murray/Animals Animals/Earth Scenes; B43(t): Tom & Therisa Stack/Tom Stack & Associates; B44(1): Stephen J. Krasemann/DRK Photo; B44(2): Doug Perrine/DRK Photo; B44(3): Nora & Rick Bowers/The Wildlife Collection; B44(4): Ed Wheeler/The Stock Market; B44(a): Stephen J. Krasemann/DRK Photo; B44(b): John Kaprielian/Photo Researchers, Inc.; B44(c): Randy Morse/Tom Stack & Associates; B44(d): Michael Seward/Peter Arnold, Inc.; B44(e): Daniel J. Cox/Natural Exposures;

UNIT C
C02-3: Tom McHugh/Photo Researchers, Inc.; C03(inset): D. Cavagnaro/DRK Photo; C05: Jeremy Woodhouse/DRK Photo; C06: Michael Groen Photography; C07(l): Ted Horowitz/The Stock Market; C07(r): Myrleen Ferguson/Photo Edit; C09: Dr. E. R. Degginger; C10: Peter Beck/The Stock Market; C11(l): Ray Pfortner/ Peter Arnold, Inc.; C11(r): O.S.F./ Animals Animals/Earth Scenes; C13: Michael Groen Photography; C14-15: Michael Groen Photography; C16(t): U.S. Geological Survey; C18(1, 2, 3 & d): Michael Groen Photography; C18(b): Paul E. Jones/Gamma-Liaison International; C18(c): Larry Ulrich/DRK Photo; C20-21: Carr Clifton/Minden Pictures; C23: Myrleen Ferguson/Photo Edit; C24(l): Gary Withey/Bruce Coleman Inc.; C24(r): Tom Stack/Tom Stack & Associates; C25(l): Michael Groen Photography; C25(r): Runk/Schoenberger/Grant Heilman Photography, Inc.; C27: Bob Daemmrich Photography; C28(bl): Michael P. Gadomski/Photo Researchers, Inc.; C28(br): Matt Bradley/Tom Stack & Associates; C28(tl): Michael Deyoung/Uniphoto; C29(bl): Julie Houck/Uniphoto; C31: Donald Nausbaum/Tony Stone Images; C32(b): John Kaprielian/Photo Researchers, Inc.; C32-33: Uniphoto; C33(br): Michael Groen Photography; C33(c): Vincent De Witt/Stock Boston; C34: Michael Groen Photography; C35(b-c): Stephen Ogilvy/ Picture It; C35(t): Uniphoto; C36(a): Michael Gadomski/Photo Researchers, Inc.; C36(m & b): Michael de Young/Uniphoto; C36(c): Matt Bradley/Tom Stack & Associates; C36(d): Claude Guillaumin/Tony Stone Images; C36(e): Darrell Gulin/DRK Photo; C36(f): Myrleen FergusonPhoto Edit; C36(l): Myrleen Ferguson/ Photo Edit; C36(r): John Kaprielian/Photo Researchers, Inc.;

UNIT D
2-3: Keith Kent/Science Source/Photo Researchers, Inc.; D03(inset): Carl Wolinsky/Stock Boston; D05: Stephen Ogilvy/Picture It ; D05(bkgd): Robert Brenner/Photo Edit; D06(bl): Michael Newman MR/Photo Edit; D06(br): Richard Price/FPG International; D06(tl): J & M Studios/Gamma-Liaison International; D06(tr): Timothy Shonnard/Tony Stone Images; D07(br): Gale Zucker/Stock Boston; D07(ttl): Rudi Von Briel/Photo Edit; D09: Dale Spartas/Gamma-Liaison International; D09(inset): Michael Groen Photography; D10(bl& tr): Michael Groen Photography; D10(c): Stephen Ogilvy/Picture It; D10(tl): Joe Sohm/Image Works; D11: Richard Hutchings/Picture It; D13: Terje Rakke/Image Bank; D13(t): Michael Groen Photography; D14(insets): Michael Groen Photography; D14-15: Gene Peach/Gamma-Liaison International; D15(t): Everett Johnson/Frozen Images; D17: Joe McDonald/Visuals Unlimited; D17(bkgd): Michael Dwyer/Stock Boston; D20: Richard Hutchings/Picture It; D21: The Granger Collection, NY ; D22(2): Bob Daemmrich/Stock Boston; D22(3): Jim Scourletis/Index Stock Photography, Inc.; D22(4): Michael Groen Photography; D24-25: Tom Bean/DRK Photo; D25(l): Robert Ginn/Photo Edit; D25(r): Barbara Cushman Rowell/DRK Photo; D27(b): Mark Reinstein/Uniphoto; D27(cl, cr, tl, tr): Jan Halaska/Photo Researchers, Inc.; D28(b): E. Webber/Visuals Unlimited; D28(c): Uniphoto; D28(tr): Ping Amranand/Uniphoto; D29(br): Jane Burton/Bruce Coleman Inc.; D29(tl): Gregory K. Scott/Photo Researchers, Inc.; D29(tr): Sonda Dawes/Image Works; D31(b): D. Young-Wolff/Masterfile; D32(c): Gay Bumgarner/Tony Stone Images; D32(l): J.C. Carton/Bruce Coleman Inc.; D32(r): Nigel Cattlin/Photo Researchers, Inc.; D33(bl): M. P. Kahl/DRK Photo; D33(tr): Tom Brakefield/Bruce Coleman Inc.; D35(b): Paul Barton/The Stock Market; D36(bl): Alan L. Detrick/Photo Researchers, Inc.; D36(br): Laura Riley/Bruce Coleman Inc.; D36(tl): Frank Siteman/Stock Boston; D36-37: Henry R. Fox/Animals Animals Earth Scenes; D37: William J. Weber/Visuals Unlimited; D39(b): Bill Horsman/Stock Boston; D40(b): L. West/Photo Researchers, Inc.; D40(t): W.A. Banaszewski/Visuals Unlimited; D41: Karl & Steve Maslowski/Photo Researchers, Inc.; D41: N. Benvie/Animals Animals /Earth Scenes; D42(all)/ / Photograph by Ansel Adams. ©1998 by the Trustees of the Ansel Adams Publishing Rights Trust. All Rights Reserved; D44(2a-c): Jan Halaska/Photo Researchers, Inc.; D44(3): Ping Amranand/Uniphoto; D44(4): D. Young-Wolff/ Photo Edit; D44(5): Paul Barton/The Stock Market; D44(6): Bill Horsman/Stock Boston; D44(tcl): Richard Hutchings/Photo Researchers, Inc.; D44(tcr): David Lissy/Index Stock Photography, Inc.; D44(tl): Gish/Monkmeyer Press; D44(tr): Tony Casper/Index Stock Photography, Inc.; D45(t): Michael Groen Photography

UNIT E
E10: Michael Groen Photography; E14-15: Michael Groen Photography; E18-19(l): Stephen Ogilvy/Picture It; E19(r): Michael Groen Photography; E21: Stephen Ogilvy/Picture It; E22(b): Stephen Ogilvy/Picture It; E22(t) & 23: Michael Groen Photography; E26(bl): Chris Sorensen /The Stock Market; E26(br): Will McCoy/Rainbow; E26(t): Stephen Ogilvy/Picture It; E27: Kathy Tarantola/Index Stock Photography, Inc.; E28(b): Michael Groen Photography; E28(t): Beatrice Hatala/RMN/Musee Picasso, Paris; E29: Tony Freeman/Photo Edit; E30(2): Stephen Ogilvy/Picture It; E30(3): Joseph Nettis/Stock Boston; E30(4): Michael Groen Photography; E30(5): Stephen Ogilvy/Picture It; E30(6): Kathy Tarantola/Index Stock Photography, Inc.; E30(tc): Stephen Ogilvy/Picture It; E30(tl): Michael Groen Photography; E31: Michael Groen Photography; E32-33: Papolla/Photo Edit; E35: M. Timothy O'Keefe/Bruce Coleman Inc.; E36: Uniphoto; E39: Steve Solum/Bruce Coleman Inc.; E40: Michael Groen Photography; E41: Brian Parker/Tom Stack & Associates; E43: Sanford/Agliolo/The Stock Market; E44(bl): Michael Groen Photography; E44(c): Phil Degginger/Bruce Coleman Inc.; E44(tr): Richard Megna/Fundamental Photographs; E45: Peter Angelo Simon/The Stock Market; E47: Steven Felsch/Wernher Krutein/Gamma-Liaison International; E48: Stephen Ogilvy/Picture It; E50: courtesy of Jetta Schantz; E52(a): Margaret Miller/Photo Researchers, Inc.; E52(b & tl): Michael Groen Photography; E52(tr): Phil Degginger/Bruce Coleman Inc.; E53: Michael Groen Photography

UNIT F
F02-3: D. Cavagnaro/DRK Photo; F03(inset): Michael Fogden/Animals Animals/Earth Scenes; F05: Michael Groen Photography; F06(t): Shellie Nelson/Unicorn Stock Photos; F07: Stephen Ogilvy/Picture It; F09: Jeff Greenberg/Unicorn Stock Photos; F10(tl): Chris Noble/Tony Stone Images; F10(tr): Michael Groen Photography; F10-11(b): Addison Geary/Stock Boston; F11(c): Michael Groen Photography; F11(tr): Ed Harp/Unicorn Stock Photos; F13: Michael Groen Photography; F14-15: Richard Hutchings/Picture It; F16-17(b): Stephen Ogilvy/Picture It; F17(t): Kimberly Burnham/Unicorn Stock Photos; F20: Richard Hutchings/Picture It; F21: Michael Groen Photography; F23: Chuck Savage/The Stock Market; F24(c): Jeff Greenberg/Visuals Unlimited; F24(tr): Don Mason/The Stock Market; F25(b): Stephen Ogilvy/Picture It; F25(t): Leslye Borden/Photo Edit; F26(t): Eric Bouvet/Gamma-Liaison International; F28: Chuck Savage /The Stock Market; F28(a): Chris Noble/Tony Stone Images; F28(c): Shellie Nelson/Unicorn Stock Photos; F28(t): David Madison/Bruce Coleman Inc.; F29: Michael Groen Photography; F30-31: Papolla/Photo Edit; F33: Michael Groen Photography; F34: Peter Cade/Tony Stone Images; F34(inset): Michael Groen Photography; F35(tr): Breck P. Kent/Animals Animals / Earth Scenes; F36-37 & 39: Michael Groen Photography; F40: Stephen Ogilvy/Picture It; F41: Richard Megna/Fundamental Photographs; F43: Stephen Ogilvy/Picture It; F44: Michael Groen Photography; F47: Arthur R. Hill/Visuals Unlimited; F48: Stephen Ogilvy/Picture It; F49: Sal Dimarco/Black Star/Harcourt; F51(t): Adrienne Hart-Davis/Photo Researchers, Inc.; F52: Michael Groen Photography; F52(a-b): Stephen Ogilvy/Picture It; F53(tl): Michael Groen Photography; F53(ml): Richard Megna/Fundamental Photographs; F53(b): Kiribati/The Stock Market

All other photographs by Harcourt photographers listed below, © Harcourt:
Weronica Ankarom, Bartlett Digital Photography, Victoria Bowen, Eric Camdem, Digital Imaging Group, Charles Hodges, Ken Karp, Ken Kinzie, Ed McDonald, Sheri O'Neal, Terry Sinclair

Illustration Credits
Michael Maydak B11; Tim Haggerty C17; Corbert Gauthier D18-19; Margarita Cruz E14-15; Rachel Geswaldo (electronic art) F16-17.